# Praise for The Inside Guide

"Michael DiPietro and Marcey Donnelly have written what I consider to be a really valuable book full of deep truth and wisdom to put the power of their approach in the hands of readers. It is much deeper, more holistic, more profound than most of what other practitioners do. This is really important work and so many people are in need of it"
~Jack Canfield, coauthor of *Chicken Soup for the Soul*

"We hear so often that 'the answer lies within,' but it is rare that someone offers such a detailed road map and guidebook for making that interior journey. The soul is sometimes compared to a spectrum, sometimes a labyrinth, sometimes a jungle. What we need to make our own journey through the spectrum of consciousness are 'soul doctors,' folks who have made their own inner journey. Only they can help us understand the why of the journey, as well as offer a field guide. If they can't do the work for us or make the entire journey with us, they can be there at the beginning and the end and cheer us on all the way through. Michael and Marcey are such guides. They offer wise advice and encouragement in this *Inside Guide* that explores so many aspects of the journey to inner development—from finding the reason we were born to removing the conditioning that keeps us from being our full true selves."
~Cyprian Consiglio, author of *Spirit, Soul, Body*

"*The Inside Guide* is a book for... you! No matter where you are on your spiritual journey, this book will help you move forward and gain new perspectives. It is like having a treasure map to follow and the treasure is inside of you. On this path of life and learning, having a roadmap is incredibly helpful. *The Inside Guide* has exercises for you to work through to create changes in perspective. Some of the concepts may be new or ideas you have worked with previously, yet, taking a look again is always beneficial. We all have internal work to do and having *The Inside Guide* to help is the most effective way to do it. In the end, it's similar to a treasure map. Finding the treasure inside you ... x marks the spot."
~Chellie Kammermeyer, Assistant Director of Licensed Teachers (ICRT), Owner of Inner Compass Reiki

"*The Inside Guide* is a comprehensive compendium of the tools and techniques for personal development and transformation. Superbly organized, divided into sections that address Mind, Body, and Spirit, *The Inside Guide* brings together many methods and strategies for change. The book follows a well-organized and clearly thought-out progression, from considering our individual journeys of self-discovery to reaching a profound understanding of our unity with the greater universe. Seekers after self-knowledge will find the book a wonderful companion on the way to deep awareness."

~Stephen Billias, coauthor of *Pilgrim Maya* (with Bela Breslau), author of *A Book of Fields* and *The American Book of the Dead*

# THE INSIDE GUIDE

Molly,

Thank you for being such a ray of light for Cliff and I, then introducing to the Hay House Writers Community. It's been an amazing journey! ♡

Marcus Donnelly

# THE
# INSIDE
# GUIDE

## Breaking Through to
## Intuitive Wisdom & Inspired Living

# Michael DiPietro
## with Marcey Donnelly

*Dedicated to the Spirit within each of us and to all the seekers and guides on the inner journey. Most especially this is dedicated to our amazing friends and family who have supported us throughout the journey of making this book a reality.*

# TABLE OF CONTENTS

# Preface

The culture we live in subtly trains us to look outside ourselves for our answers, our success and our satisfaction in life. We have become conditioned by our fixation on the external world. Because of this we create distance from our true center, a "light" that has always been there but seems to be hidden deep within. Here is something many of us understand but few experience: this light inside is the only place where you can find your well-being.

Painful experiences, such as depression and anxiety, seem common for many people these days. With the difficulties that are happening in the world, life may seem more uncertain than ever. But much of our experience can change in a positive lasting way, when we learn to go inward and touch our deeper truths.

In this book you will learn how your mind and your consciousness actually work to create your experiences. Once you have this key, you can breakthrough your obstacles from within and create more useful and profound experiences for yourself—and your life. The purpose is to put you behind the wheel, and to empower you to make your own clear choices and to be your own guide.

This book is meant to remind you that everything starts within. Our intention is to take you through an inner journey, to help you to dig deep and to reach your center. At times it might be challenging because looking inside also means seeing the shadows, those parts of ourselves we would rather keep hidden. However, with the guidance and tools you are about to encounter, you will be able to experience a sense of peace, clarify your way, and create your inspired life with purpose.

You could think of this book as an intimate journal. How it integrates into your life is personal. This is *your* story. We will discuss a process that is meant to support and guide you in becoming more fulfilled. The execution and the impact will vary based on your own experiences—and on how deep you are willing to go. While this is a guide, the actual effects and changes you will see as a reader are personal, yet well beyond what you might think is possible.

With this guide you can learn to look inward to create your life of inspiration, meaning and purpose. It will support you to find your inner answers, get through your obstacles and ultimately shine brightly in the world.

This is your Inside Guide.

# Introduction

## The Benefits of Going Inward

There is a profound need for human beings to go inward, even though it is often not recognized or supported by our western and externalized society. What is this need? Why does it seem that some people do fine without it? Does one really *need* to go inward?

Okay, maybe at a personal level it is not a need but a choice. Then the better questions may be:

"What are the benefits of going inward?"

"What will I gain by doing this?"

"How specifically is it going to benefit me to look inward?"

"Is it worth it?"

As an example: if someone needs a strategy for building their business or career, how is it going to benefit them to look inward? They could put a strategy in place with external goals, but if they are struggling with motivation, or with fear, or with any other of the internal experiences that can impede the outer strategy, these factors are going to make a huge difference in their success.

If you look within and embark on the journey of finding your answers, of overcoming your obstacles, and of living your purpose: it is going to open doors and opportunities that you might not fathom in your practical mind. Open doors and opportunities— why wouldn't someone want that? What is possible? Well-being? Satisfaction? Peace? Success? How do you define what is possible when there are so many possibilities? Creating a single definition for any one person limits all other possibilities. Thus, it remains for you, the individual reader, to discover for yourself.

The journey offered through this book is different. By picking up this book, you may think or feel that something is missing, or there is a gap between who you are and who you want to be. You may have been having a hard time with getting along, not feeling fulfilled or not finding joy and peace. You have probably read other books where one can get to a place of some empowerment. But in my experience, most approaches got me to some peak experience, and then the old patterns came back quickly when I came back to my everyday life. That is when enlightenment fades and normal patterns replace the feeling of the peak experience. All of the books, conference notes, and meditation insights get tossed back into the closet when normal life kicks back in. I call this dynamic, of having peak experiences and living your everyday life, reaching the mountaintop and the return to the village.

The magic of this book is that it is your own mountaintop enlightenment itself that guides you—as your unique, amazing self—back to the village. It is the mountaintop enlightenment that shows you how to replace your old outdated patterns, and to trust the wisdom that has always been inside you and has been waiting for you to see.

Is there more to taking this journey of going farther inward?

Yes, because going inward is the only way to wake up. This is about your awakening to something more within yourself. There is a quote by Carl Jung: "Who looks outside dreams; who looks inside awakens."

Even though reading this book will benefit you in unique ways, to do so is optional. It remains a choice and much depends on your choices in life. Since waking up is optional, you might choose to go on being asleep and sleepwalking through life. But if you want to know who you really are, if you want to find your inner light, if you want to awaken; you have to go inward. During this inner journey, you will unravel a lot of self-limiting patterns that get in the way. Put simply, if you face your internal world, it is going to make your life better. Sometimes positive changes might be evident right away, sometimes not, but they will emerge eventually. A good way to look at this is like an investment strategy, but it is investing in who you are and the profit is a more fulfilling life. This process guides you to living out the life that you were born to lead. Remember, you are the only one who can do this.

There also has to be a trust that this is going to lead you somewhere. That trust is also within you. In the beginning when I first started meditating, there were no guarantees it was going to do anything. I would sometimes ask myself, "Why the heck am I doing this? It seems ridiculous." But once you begin to look inward as a lifestyle, and let go of the need to achieve anything, that's when real progress happens. I wanted to be "enlightened" when I first started. "I want to be enlightened! I need enlightenment!" What the heck is that? The mental grasping was so counterproductive. I now have an understanding of it, but it did not come until years later and only after letting go of grasping for it.

So if it comes down to personal choice, where does the need come in? It comes into play when we consider the collective level of human experience.

## The Collective Need

We have discussed how looking within is a choice on the personal level. However, there is a real need when we examine the collective level, and we are all part of the collective. Humanity needs to evolve, else we are not going to make it with the challenges that confront us. Additionally, there is rampant dysfunction and codependency that operates internally, and keeps many people disempowered and bound in patterns that hold them back.

Once enough people are awake, then it will begin to become a collective awakening for most of humanity. Then it gets easier for more and more people to get onboard. A collective awakening… it's what we need as a species. This book is a step in that direction.

For example, there are things that took me years to get my head around and to work with. Now I notice some people in their 20's for whom those same things are simply common, such as understanding relationship dynamics or a deeper awareness of the spiritual nature of life. They seem to get it naturally. In a way, we are building on the evolution of humanity as time goes on. We are building consciousness so that each generation that comes along will benefit from the work that the previous generation has done. With that we need to wake up because we are getting faced with some bigger challenges (for instance, climate change, pandemics, wars, economic disparity, ideological polarization, disruptions in governments, humanitarian disasters, etc.). Events are occurring that are pushing the edge for people and there are not a lot of tools on how to get through it. However, once we start to work collectively, when it is more "we" versus "me", that is where the real need occurs and our true purpose can be fulfilled.

Let's discuss a bit about this book and how it's designed to support you on your inner journey.

## How This Book Is Organized—The Power of the Three Parts

There are three main parts to this book:

Part 1 is *Finding Your Answers.*

Part 2 is *Overcoming Your Obstacles.*

Part 3 is *Living Your Purpose.*

Each of the three parts builds on each other in a progressive fashion. The further you read, the deeper the content goes. Each part has a theme and a guiding question.

## About the Three Themes

In Part One, "Finding Answers", the theme is "Mind." In addition to exploring and understanding the mind, we look at our whole identity structure and how this is created. We provide models for better understanding our minds and for how our consciousness operates. Part One has to do more with the mind and how the mind plays into this work. Finding Answers is not only about the mind, but also for the mind and its need for understanding (though we find our deeper answers in the body).

In Part Two, "Overcoming Obstacles", we venture into the experiential path. The theme is "Body" where we explore physiology and neurology in order to understand how we create and can change the experience of our obstacles. Part Two is more focused on the body and on our physiology. Here we get down to the felt experience, to what is happening in the brain at the level of physiology, and to the importance of being grounded in the body. A much deeper aspect of this section has to do with the unconscious mind—the parts of your experiences of which you are unaware. In Part Two we explore deeply how the unconscious mind relates to the body and the brain, as well as how these come together in the creation and transformation of obstacles you might be facing.

Part Three is "Living Purpose." The theme is "Spirit." In this part we discuss going beyond the self and experiencing our part in a greater unitive consciousness. This opens the door to knowing your purpose and integrating your mountaintop experiences into your everyday life.

In the three themes, we have Mind-Body-Spirit. Now, body, mind, and spirit are actually all one, but for the sake of being able to talk about them, we will temporarily separate them into three.

We can also categorize the sections as: Conscious, Unconscious, and Superconscious.

To describe these terms, consider the metaphor of an iceberg. Part One is the conscious mind (what we see above the surface), Part Two is the unconscious mind (the part hidden below the surface), and Part Three is the super- conscious (the ocean itself...a  metaphor for the eternal mystery where all is one in a unified field of consciousness). The iceberg and the ocean are both water, just in different forms and thus appearing different.

A final way to look at the sectioning is...

1. The journey inward.

2. Deeper on that journey inward.

3. As far as one could go inward, beyond which nothing can be defined.

Underlying the different ways of classifying the sections is a basic tripartite structure. The Taoist would say Yin, Yang, and Tao. This structure is any of the ways in which we have an arbitrary polarity, contained and transcended in a third state. Basically, we have a "+", and we have a "−", then we have the "space" that holds the + and −.

Is there an importance in the order of the themes of the parts? Yes.

The reason it starts with the mind first is because that is generally where most people are oriented. Most of us want to understand something before we jump in with both feet. If we jumped right into the body, it would be more difficult to understand because the body remembers and reflects the unconscious mind. We have to first introduce the structures of mind, and then we can go deeper and explore the body—as it relates to the unconscious content of the mind. If we have not introduced mind first, then we do not have a basis for our content in section two.

We proceed through the book in the following order: the mind, to body, to spirit. Much of the time it is our mind that is getting in the way, so in that respect the body is closer to spirit than mind. Yet spirit runs through your mind and your body (the body-mind), thus spirit is not separate from either (also mind is not separate from body).

We talk about the distinctions between mind and body, mind and spirit, or body and spirit, but that is only to give us a sense of how they differ. In actuality they are unified into a totality. Thus, in order to understand we break the distinctions apart; we talk about them, and then in the end we put them back together again.

## About the Three Guiding Questions

Each part of the book, along with the three themes, has a guiding question that goes along with it. These are meant as a background guide, another aspect of the three-part structure.
These three questions are:

- ▸ Who are you?
- ▸ What are you?
- ▸ What are you really here to do?

The three questions provide a backdrop throughout the book. They are woven into the themes and content. These are large over-arching questions, and they have a different quality to them. They are not meant to be answered immediately, but through a process of unfolding within you, throughout your life. Throughout the book, there are also numerous other questions we will ask as part of the process. We will refer to those as inquiry questions. They are different in nature than the three guiding questions. The three guiding questions are very impactful for us to explore as human beings. They can be daunting for some people, so it helps to remember that the answers can take time to unfold.

## Reading This Book Effectively

This book is structured in a progressive format so that each section builds on itself. We recommend reading the book in a linear fashion and not hopping ahead. Each part is creating a foundation for the next, building as it goes.

We would also like to suggest that readers use the book on their own terms. None of this is set in stone. If part of the content is not usable for you personally, then throw it out, and take only the pieces that work for you. The way to check that is to go inside, and check with yourself about whether it makes sense for you, or not. Does it resonate? Is it helpful? Does it bring an "Aha!" moment? Is it guiding you in the right direction?

However, once in a while you might resist some of the content. Sometimes this is because there is something in your unconscious that you must face. Each of us must discern for ourselves: Is it resistance from hitting an "inner button" or is it simply not useful? Generally, you can tell it is resistance if there is a reaction. Only you can gauge this for yourself.

Please always remember that you are in charge of the process. Even though this book is a guide, the true guide is within you and always inviting you deeper.

## About the Authors

### Michael's Path

Like many others, I went to school and got a formal college education. In my twenties, I had a kind of crisis moment where I realized my career in technical sales didn't fulfill me. I had to ask the questions that are asked in this book: *Who am I? What am I here to do? What is my purpose?* I started exploring.

I also asked, *"if I was to be of service to others, how would I want to do that?"* I thought of getting a master's degree, but at that age I wanted to jump into something as fast as possible. I was fascinated by massage, bodywork, and energy work so these were my first entrée into the healing arts.

Along the way I studied a progression of modalities. First, I became a certified massage therapist and learned a number of different bodywork and healing techniques. Then I got into meditation, then martial arts and then into Neuro Linguistic Programming (NLP). As I learned more, I used the tools for my own process of learning and development. I also asked myself, *"How can I best apply these modalities in the service of others?"*

With my intuitive gifts as well as the trainings, I became more effective at working with people, refining my process as I went along. When the coaching field was emerging, I started a professional coaching practice and eventually worked for a number of years as a business and executive coach in San Francisco. Though I was successful, at a certain point it no longer felt correct for me.

I had another crisis at midlife where I wanted a different life. I wanted to move out of the big city and use different approaches with my work, so I left everything and retooled my work to have the more spiritual format that it has today. Every crisis point is best taken as an opportunity, right? We either walk through the door or we do not.

## Marcey's Path

I was introduced to Michael by a special family member who knew I would appreciate the psychological, physiological, and spiritual approach that he offered. After working one-one-one with him for several years (and through many break-through Aha! moments), I got to a point where I wanted to do something more. While I was secure and living a great life with my husband and kids, I had this calling to keep exploring other opportunities to connect with others. I had been a business professional working in finance, but always had other interests from professional home organizing to volunteering in parent/teacher associations, women's leadership, youth development, and owning a franchise. I loved working with others, but felt that my more spiritual experiences were my passion. I am Reiki trained and spent many hours as a conference attendee or volunteer for Hay House, with the chance to listen to the most amazing speakers, while continuing my own transformation. This was my happy place.

In April 2021, amidst the disorder of the pandemic, I got the call. "Marcey, this is Michael. Do you want to write a book with me?" This was the doorway to my "something more."

Michael and I would not be here now if we had not listened to our Inside Guides, investigated, gotten curious, and pulled the thread to see what was next.

## How We Wrote This Book

We wrote this book in a unique way. Most of the content was generated by transcribed conversations between Michael and Marcey. A majority of the conversational aspect has been edited out, but at times throughout the book, we found it useful to leave the conversation in place. You might notice "MARCEY" or "MICHAEL," referenced throughout the book. This indicates who is speaking and are the areas where the original conversational format was left in place.

We are both so glad you decided to read this book. It brings us great joy knowing this work is out in the world and that you will benefit from what we have created. But now it's time to put the focus on you and your inner journey.

Welcome to Part One: Finding Answers.

Part One

# FINDING ANSWERS

CHAPTER 1

▲ ▲ ▲

# The Source Within You

## The Start of a Magical Journey

Welcome to the wonderful world inside you! You are about to embark on an epic journey of conscious awareness and transformation of your interior life. This journey will also bring you to another dimension of yourself—a "something more" factor which can guide you in a mystical and magical way from within. The inner work that this book offers can bring you to that door, but only you can walk through it and reach your center.

## Reaching Your Center, The Source

When you reach your center, you also reach the source for what you want in your life. It does not mean you go without challenges, but your center is the source of your success and well-being.

At some point that journey to finding your center becomes very personal and specific to your life. For one person it could be feeling a connection with God. For another person it could be reaching a place of silence and stillness. For another it could be spending time alone in nature. In Buddhist terminology we would call it reaching the void, reaching emptiness or Sunyata. In mystical Christianity it is the unitive experience or an experience of God. In the Sufi tradition it is called Fana.

So how does one begin to experience their center?

## A Journey of Self-Discovery

To get to your center it has to be a journey of self-discovery. One of the ancient Greek maxims is "Know thyself". (Although Goethe, the famed German writer, had said, "Know thyself? If I knew myself I'd run away.") In this whole concept of "knowing of self", we need to see our light. We also have to see our shadow and not run away from it.

Some people run away from self-discovery because it is not an easy quick fix, as so many Western-minded people want.

We need to learn that not everything is going to happen right away. The journey of self-discovery is a lifestyle choice. It is a journey to reach your center and to wake up to what is really going on—on the inside. It is the journey toward your own loving nature.

## You are the Inner Love That Can Never Be Defined

We are all moving toward love. That is one of the main goals of this approach: to move toward an inner love, so you know yourself as love. At the end of the day these experiences we seek—the better life, the better relationship, or whatever it may be—it comes down to love. It is an inner love. It is that mystery of who you are. That is the end goal, if there is one. It is to know yourself as love, as that mystery. It is to know not only that you are loved and lovable as you are, but that you are actually love and you defy definition.

Some people might see inner love as fluff or as not powerful. Then they would be missing the point entirely. Again, this love is a mystery. We have to make a distinction when we talk about this dimension of love. In this context we are not talking about love romantically or emotionally. We are talking about love as the backdrop that allows us to be alive. It is the allowing, inclusive, accepting part of ourselves. In and of itself, this love is like the vastness of space, allowing all the objects in the universe to be as they are.

You cannot say, "here is love", or "there is love", because as a mystery it cannot be grasped. It involves caring and wanting the best for everyone. Yet it is not only caring about and having empathy for others, but for ourselves as well. It is always moving us in the direction of wellness to the greater well-being of everyone. Love wants everyone to be well. If someone is not, love says, "Okay, I love you, no matter what—unconditionally and completely."

Love is waiting for each of us to wake up to this part of ourself, and it is eternally patient in that wait. It does not have an agenda. It simply says, "Okay, live out your life and I will accept and love you no matter what occurs for you." Unconditional love. It is all inclusive.

Imagine if you could apply that to your experiences. Maybe you get broadsided by some painful experience. When you are identified with love, it might hurt, but there is a place for solace, a place for nurturing, a place for respite. It is a helpful place for when life might not be ideal. As an example: if someone lost their arm, that would be a terrible thing to occur. But love would say, "Okay, you are still whole and complete. You are lovable. You can give and receive love." Nothing is missing in love!

Love is like the sun coming up today. It is something you can count on and something that is a part of everyone. It is also something each of us must find and experience in our own unique way. Understanding your own journey to this love and how to live it in your everyday life is key to your success. The following metaphor is a theme for people's spiritual journey. It runs throughout this book as an important reference point for you to make progress on your path.

## The Journey to the Mountaintop and the Return to the Village

The mountaintop represents our retreat from everyday life and the clarity of enlightenment. We go to the mountaintop to have our spiritual experiences. The return to the village is the integration back into our everyday life of whatever spiritual experiences we have had on the mountaintop. That aspect, that return, is where a lot of people hit challenges.

**KEY CONCEPT**

*Mountaintop clarity is available in everyday life*

We will discuss this more in Part Three, but it is important to understand that this book helps people make that journey back to the village. It gives them a roadmap not only for reaching their mountaintop, but just as importantly, for integrating their spiritual awakenings into their everyday life.

Sometimes this mountaintop spirituality seems like a switch; it is either on or off. However, it could be an energy, or a connection that resonates and lives with you throughout the day. The mountaintop concept—this feeling of pure peace, love, or stillness—is something most of us have felt at some point. Everyone has this inside themselves. Recall a time when you felt at peace or in flow with life. It could be when you felt very connected to spirit or to God. Maybe it was being part of a spiritual community of likeminded people.

Maybe as a parent, it was holding your child for the first time. Maybe it was a time in nature, or while on a retreat or spending time with friends. Maybe for no reason whatsoever, you felt peace in your body, or a calmness of mind or a spirit of unconditional love. These moments may have felt sacred, or special, but seem forgotten when we get back into everyday life. Not only is there an opportunity to have this energy in our regular village life, but also this is a very powerful place to live from. How one gets there and what it looks like is uniquely coded for everyone individually.

On the mountaintop we are one with everything. As we return to the village, we do so through our authentic individuality. As the mountaintop awareness translates through one's individuality, it is not experienced by everyone in the same way. Also, it may fade as time goes on. But once we have had the experience and understand it, we can begin to live it more authentically. First, we each need to truly understand what the mountaintop is. We can gain more experience with this through retreats and quiet time. But our society with its continual external focus and preference for "busy-ness" does not readily support this.

While there are multiple established ways to get to the mountaintop, few seem adept at guiding us back to the village. That journey needs to be personal to you. You make that return to the village through the uniqueness of who you are. When you do this you remain engaged in your life, but in a way that is informed by the mountaintop.

This part of the book is about the workings of your mind and finding your answers, but before diving deeper into that, there are a few important topics to cover at the onset. These next topics help deepen the invitation to your interior life. You could think of them as a primer to doing the inner work.

CHAPTER 2

▲ ▲ ▲

# The Deeper Invitation to Go Inward

## Nothing Is Broken, Nothing Needs Fixing

*"One of the most striking moments was hearing for the first time that there was nothing about me that was broken or needed to be fixed."*
~Client

It is significant to discuss this at the very beginning. What we are affirming by saying "nothing is broken, nothing needs fixing", is a reference point for your wholeness—for your completeness.

Take a moment, close your eyes and take a deep breath. Tell yourself the following phrase: "There is nothing about who I am that is broken or needs fixing. I am whole and complete in this moment." What do you notice when you say this to yourself?

This is a powerful concept because part of the problem is that many people erroneously believe that something is wrong with them. Yet, nothing is actually wrong with them. They are running neural pathways and mental programs that have predictable outcomes. A program could have an outcome that causes someone to believe that something is wrong with them. That erroneous belief is what gets debunked from the very start. We want to understand this right up front. We can transform self-limiting mental programs, but always within the concept of being whole and complete—not needing fixing, because "you" are not broken.

Someone could be having an especially painful experience that makes them feel broken. But in reality, the being of them is not broken. It is their mind and their programming of that particular experience that has caused them to feel and believe it to be so. The brain is working properly to get that particular outcome of believing in brokenness, but it is not true.

Even though we are whole, we want to address any limiting programs and transform them. Our wholeness is the backdrop that builds rapport and creates a space of acceptance. We enter into transformation with this concept of wholeness. It is the ending point, but it is also the starting point. Let us say a little bit more on the "broken" myth as it occurs on a psychological level.

Many of us have encountered some type of pain or trauma in our past. Maybe some of us are presently going through something difficult. Trauma comes in many forms and varieties, so it helps to not make assumptions about our own or others' experiences. When pain or trauma occurs, one of the things that can happen is a fracturing of our identity into parts. The fracture and the parts tend to stay hidden. Fractured parts do not interact and may have different agendas. This is one instance where people tend to feel as though they are broken or something needs fixing because the original trauma created a fracture or a pain point in their psyche (discussed later in Part One).

There is a process for unifying these parts back together again, but we have to posit that the wholeness is there at the beginning and is containing the fractured parts. Though it might feel like a broken experience for someone, it is still occurring in their wholeness. We are always whole and complete—no matter what.

It is very important to know what you believe about yourself. When people unconsciously believe they are broken, then they get to work on it. They may think, "Something is wrong with me and I have to fix it." That belief then becomes the motivation to do the inner work. When we debunk that belief at the beginning, it pulls the carpet out from under the belief in brokenness. Once we do that, the motivation will need to come from somewhere else within us.

Let's take a look now at some greater motivation for looking inward.

## Toward a Greater Well-Being

Toward a greater well-being, that is what we are all aiming for. As human beings we want to be well physically, mentally, emotionally and spiritually. WELL-BEING. That is your natural state of being, the one you were born with. Throughout our lives we have experienced pain and challenges. Our problems and our attempts to solve them have created a type of conditioning that keeps us from our deeper well-being. Conditioning causes us to operate in a way that is not authentic to our true being, such as people pleasing or acting aggressively towards others.

Well-being has always been there but it got covered beneath layers of conditioning. Conditioning is like having dirty windows. Well-being is the light shining through the windows. But if the windows are covered with layers of dirt, then less light comes through. One must clean the dirt off in order for the light to shine through. You are not the dirt—you are the light!

Can you think of the word well-being as a verb rather than as a noun? It is not about something to get to; it is more about the choices we make in how we live our lives. Am I going to live in a "well" way? In a wealthy way? It is not just financial wealth as in money, but also internal wealth. It is about feeling abundant in who we are. If you want to "achieve" well-being, it is a process. It is a verb. It is an unfolding.

## What are Nominalizations and another way to look at well-being?

Nominalizations are verbs that we turn into nouns and then we think we can grab them.

Abstract words and concepts such as "empowerment" and "well-being" are actually processes that happen in real time, but sometimes we must stretch out the timespan in order to notice them unfolding. When you make these terms an end goal, they become something to achieve, something that you will or will not have right now. But you can be in that state of well-being as it unfolds over time. Feel the differentiation between well-being as something to achieve versus well-being as an action unfolding continually from the center of your being.

One could say, "I do not have that well-being right now" versus saying, "I am living in a state of unfolding well-being. I may not yet be feeling that but I can imagine what that would be like for myself."

Well-being can be a way of living life today.

Even with a life of well-being we may see or experience things within ourselves that we do not want to. This is always in the service of well-being. We might feel off our path at times, but this too is part of it. Sometimes we go down a cul-de-sac for a bit before finding our way back onto the main road of well-being.

When we say well-being, it offers more understanding by breaking it into two words—*well* and *being.*

## ☞ KEY ETYMOLOGY

*The root of the word well comes from the same root as wealth…old English wel.*

An Etymology of Wealth by Jeremy Williams

…:'Wealth' comes from the old English 'weal', which means 'wealth, welfare, and wellbeing'. Weal is in turn related to the older word 'wel', meaning 'in a state of good fortune, welfare, or happiness'. 'Wel' gives birth to 'welth' around 1250 AD, and 'welthi' a century or so later. By 1430 it seems to have settled around the idea of riches and prosperity, leaving behind the older meanings of wider wellbeing and health.

In reviewing the root of the word well, we can see the relationship to health, or wealth, to genuinely being well, but it is a wellness on multiple levels. It is mostly from the center of our being—our spiritual level. It can mean wellness whether it be physical, emotional, mental or spiritual. Even if we have a physical limitation, we can live in a wellness mindset and a wellness spirit. It is important to acknowledge that some things in our lives are experiences we simply have to come to terms with, especially when they are beyond our control. Some we can transform; some we cannot. If someone we love passes away, we cannot change that. If someone is born with a certain disability, one cannot change that. However, one can learn, adapt and grow. A "well" and abundant life is available.

The second word, "being", has to do with our essence—or that centered place within us.

Well-being is when we truly come from our center, from that core of who we truly are. Our wellness comes from the inside and ripples out into the rest of our lives.

Everyone will define well-being on their own terms. As an example: well-being may show up as a healthy body, eating right, doing meditations, paying attention to what your experiences are, fostering love, compassion in your communication with other people, joyous time with family and friends, time in prayer or a spiritual practice. These are some common definitions. Since everyone may have a different definition of what well-being is, let's ask the questions:

> *What does well-being mean to you?*

> *How do you define it?*

## Exercise

**Take some time to consider these questions. Have fun with this. Brainstorm, journal, pray, dance or use whatever method works best for you. Let your imagination play. Keep it light so that you are creating well-being as you do this exercise. Let the answers come to you whenever and however they do, for example in a dream or in a conversation with a friend. Let it be ok if for the definitions to unfold over time.**

Now that you're on a path toward defining your well-being, you are ready to consider the next very important point in awakening.

## The Magic of the Outer Reflecting the Inner & Vice Versa

*"Your outside world is a reflection of your inside world.*
*What goes on in the inside, shows on the outside."*
~Bob Proctor

"The outer reflects the inner" is a phenomenal concept. We are so externalized. Many people feel as though their outer and their inner world are different. They feel as if that which is happening inside themselves does not necessarily affect or reflect that which is happening outside of themselves. This concept is the essence of one's empowerment. Everything that is happening on the inside is being projected outwardly.

We are constantly attracting certain outer circumstances based on our inner experiences. Like it or not, the outer is a reflection of the inner. It is a reflection of what we are thinking, feeling and doing on the interior. When you realize that there is no difference and that you can change your inner experience, then you have the real key to the law of attraction; such as when negative thoughts attract negative circumstances, and positive thoughts attract positive circumstances. Much of the positive change we desire can happen with a rerouting of our neural pathways. This approach is from the field of Neuro-Linguistic Programming (NLP) and is covered more deeply in Part Two. There we provide powerful tools for shifting your world from the inside out.

Once you shift your inner experience, you can shift how you attract certain circumstances, events, people, places or things into your life based on your interior. This is really the magic of it. You are shifting things around on the inside first, then proceeding with your goals and outer strategies once that inner shift has occurred. Yes, we still have to take action in the external world. But if we do not first shift it on the inside, then we are going to be fighting against it: versus shifting it first on the inside and then letting it flow organically from the inside. Then the changes we want can happen easily and naturally.

**⚷ KEY CONCEPT**

*Our external experiences are a reflection of what is happening within us.*

For example, someone might say that they experience chaos or find a lot of negative people in their life. How would chaos and negative people on the outside reflect something on the inside?

Let's take this chaos example. We would start to look at what this person's internal experience is when chaos happens. We would start unpacking the internal experience. Maybe they feel anxiety every time the chaos happens. Then we would look, not at the chaos, but at the anxiety and the need to have that anxiety and the attachments to the inner experience. In this example, in this person's life, anxiety may attract the chaos. It gives them a reason for the anxiety. If you move them into a non-chaotic situation and the anxiety was not shifted, they would find another outer reason to give them cause for anxiety. It is always state-dependent from what is on the inside.

For instance, if someone has anger issues, they are going to attract circumstances and people and reasons that allow them to justify their anger. It is not the person outside causing them to feel the anger; it is that they have a propensity for anger and they are attracting someone who is allowing them to act that out. It is an attachment to the state, the internal state; whether it be anger, whether it be anxiety, whether it be depression. Whatever it is, that is the attractor for the so-called "circumstances."

We can begin to think of it as an "attractor pattern." It is a system. It will have its own energy. Its function is to attract certain outcomes and circumstances. If it is a negative attractor pattern, it will attract negative people and give someone a negative experience. Fortunately, it works the same way for positive patterns as well, which attract wonderful people and events to us.

The concept may seem like "the chicken or the egg" scenario... which came first? You could say that the circumstances happened, causing one to feel something; OR is it that feeling something has caused one to attract these circumstances? Regardless of which came first, thinking of it in terms of attracting is the much more useful tool. In the one scenario we are a victim of circumstance, but in the other we are a master of it. When we work with the feeling first, it can lead to a shift in the outer circumstances. The inner state attracts the outer circumstances. The magic happens when you understand that you are attracting everything in your life from the inside.

Whatever you want it starts from within! Yet often the world around us does not recognize this powerful concept. The next chapter explores a powerful yet simple concept and how it relates to the inner and outer worlds—your attention.

CHAPTER 3

# Where Is Your Attention Direction?

## Your Ability to Pay Attention–Within or Without?

Your ability to pay attention is one of your gifts. It is the ability to keep your mind on one thing, to pay attention to something, to focus and concentrate. This is a challenge for people with ADHD because their attention is moving around a lot. Even for successful multitaskers sometimes their attention is hopping from thing to thing. Your attention is also a highly valuable commodity that other people want. Everyone is trying to get your attention.

You can begin to foster the ability to pay attention not only to the objects of your attention, but more simply, that you can pay attention. It might be more difficult for some people and easier for others, but what is key here is that you are going to have to pay attention first to yourself and to your interior life.

The attention we are learning is internal noticing. We are conditioned to notice outside ourselves and to look to the world around us for what we want. But, as we pay attention, we can start to direct that attention inward. That is the attention direction; it is the ability to pay attention and to notice whether we are focused inside or outside ourself, within or without.

Paying attention to things outside of ourselves is natural. We are never internally focused 100 percent of the time. If I am doing dishes, I have to focus on what I am doing, which is external. But I could also pay attention to what I am feeling when I am doing the dishes, which is internal (which for me is usually dread. I'm joking here, but maybe there's a slight element of truth!).

But why is it often challenging to notice what is going on inside? There are many reasons, but a primary one is your attention is being marketed.

## How Our Culture Profits from Your Attention

Our culture, in its quest for the almighty dollar, has honed to a fine art the fields of marketing and advertising. The tactics used by these professions are highly manipulative and meant to capture and hold someone's attention for as long as possible. Social media in particular is now being exposed for how addicting these tactics are. It keeps you focused outside yourself…the answer lies out there if you keep searching, and scrolling, and posting, and commenting, and liking, and on and on and on. This is what they want and monetize, your constant attention. While media has it benefits and can even be enjoyable at times, too much focus on our media is a big part of the problem. As an exercise, you can explore and notice your relationship with media.

## Technology's Double Edge

Technology has also sped up the "connection" concept so that we are more aware of things that are happening around the globe in real time. It has changed many parts of our lives from how we work, to how we socialize, to understanding where our food comes from.

Yet technology is a double-edged sword. It is also creating a problem in that tech addiction keeps people distracted from looking inward. This is why a lot of people feel a kind of emptiness on the inside, because of the broken promise from our society and its technological advances. The promise is that technology will improve our life, but often it tends to disconnect us from nature and from actual human interaction. Also, the pace of life seems to be quickening with technology. Those caught in the trap feel they have to keep up. Social media adds fuel to the fire. We are finding a lot of people who are feeling unfulfilled because of it.

Through this work you learn that the only place for fulfillment is within. Scrolling through your screen faster is not going to get you there. This is a big problem for humanity. Tech is getting in the way of connecting in a real way. Yes, we are all connected, and it is connecting us easier and faster, but it is nothing like connecting when we can physically come together. It does not compare. That is the double-edged sword of technology. It is good to understand since it is so relevant to our modern-day lives. Technology is helping and hurting at the same time. So, maybe it has more to do with personal power and your personal relationship to the technology... how you use it? Is it to your detriment or to your advantage?

## Forces That Keep You Bound

A habitual external focus keeps many people captive and disempowered, but it is not entirely their fault. We have been promised the "American Dream." We have been promised that if we play a part in capitalism and consumerism, that it will pay dividends and give us what we want out of life. What a lot of people are finding out is that it is not true.

We are living with capitalism as the dominant economic model. But I call our capitalism "mutant capitalism" because it has become solely focused on profit over people. Capitalism, as it was originally laid out, was not intended to be profit over people, but to be profit and people. We can focus on profit, but not at the expense of the human being. That is where it goes mutant. There are two kinds of wealthy: the wealthy who feel as if everyone can be wealthy and there is plenty to go around, and the wealthy who feel as if "I got mine and that is what matters, even if it means stepping on others along the way." The latter is greed and it is creating disparities in our world.

While overall we have grown in consciousness, many people don't seem to see how they are being led astray. The unconscious mind can be easily manipulated. People can get misled very easily. This is what cults do. They prey on people's natural desire for love and fill that space until people become dependent on the cult and the cult leader. They are unaware that the experience is actually happening inside them. It is not happening outside themselves. This is what unscrupulous gurus do. They scoop up the love and adoration, which is meant for our own spirit, and they let their people project that love upon them. The misguided devotees think the guru is the source, when the source is in each and every one of us. Please don't misunderstand me here. There are many good sincere gurus who are not like that and are powerful spiritual guides. But some gurus manipulate people and can manipulate that place of yearning in the heart...the love within each of us that wants to be fulfilled.

These days there is a lot of spin and narrative, and that is another reason why this book is important. Much today is about story;

what is your story? What is the narrative going on? But the story does not necessarily have anything to do with the truth. If the spin doctors of media have control of the narrative, they think they can control the truth. Not so.

This work tends to sidestep the narrative because the story, or what you tell yourself, can sometimes keep you stuck in the past. The narrative can lead to a rationalization of the mind which is part of the problem. It keeps people stuck. "Well, if Joe made a million dollars, I should be able to make a million dollars too." That is the wrong kind of thinking. Instead, it could be "What does it feel like internally to have a million dollars?" Those comparisons, or looking outside ourselves, or having some sort of checklist are positions that can keep us bound.

Many people choose not to deal with their difficulties or challenges. However, these can be things that are keeping you from feeling as if you're living your best life. You are living with them and dealing with them, but by avoidance which takes a lot of energy.

But you're still dealing with it, right?

The whole thing is that you are living with the results of a certain internal orientation where it appears those results are happening on the outside. This is tied to the attention direction because we are often trained to look for the answer outside ourselves. Most people gloss over the internal stuff. They do not see that there is so much going on inside, a whole rich universe on the interior. We are trained to continually externalize and to continually look outside ourselves.

There are also certain internal processes which we self-employ that keep us from looking within. These are our own self-created methods of avoidance. Generally, these self-created methods stem from a fear of looking inward, causing us to ignore our interior life. These methods are discussed in the next chapter.

CHAPTER 4

## Avoidance and Inquiry to Looking Inward

The following methods—externalization, distraction, suppression and spiritual bypass—are typical ways in which we avoid looking inward. These methods may work for some time, but in the long run, they can be very problematic and keep us from our well-being. Let's look at them one by one.

### Externalization

Externalization starts as a means of seeking validation. It begins at a very young age as a way for children to know they are seen and heard, the validation of their existence. They are searching for a self, but they learn to do this on the outside, usually in the approval of their parents. Once the process begins, it slowly gets transferred to other areas of life over time. For those that get conditioned in this way, they perceive that the solutions and answers exist outside of them and they look to others for guidance. It could be how they act to gain attention or praise or more simply, in a continual search for the answers outside their own internal wisdom. Eventually, it keeps them from having to face what is happening within and their attention goes external.

### Distraction

Distraction is related to externalization but can happen in how we filter and modulate our internal experiences. Distraction can be anything done repeatedly that keeps one from noticing the deeper truth within. It is how we divert and waste our valuable attention. An example would be watching television when we are feeling lonely or bored. Drug and alcohol use can also be a powerful form of distraction by numbing what is actually occurring.

## Suppression

Suppression means we are trying to push an uncomfortable experience that is arising back down into the unconscious and out of awareness. An example could be when feelings of grief or shame arise and the person does not want to acknowledge the painful feelings. When we do that, it is essentially like pushing down on a spring. We try to bury it to escape from it. Keeping it pushed down takes energy to keep it out of consciousness. In essence, when we suppress, we are having to manage our environment and our reality in such a way that makes sure that the "suppressed thing" does not pop up again. It is continual energy we have to assert, as if we are constantly pushing down on that spring.

We try to push it down, but it pops up again, and we push it down, and it pops up again and again. That is how the suppression goes, like a yoyo.

In the study "Inflammation and emotion regulation: Findings from the MIDUS II" by Dr. James Gross, a psychology professor at Stanford University, it was demonstrated that the act of suppressing emotions is cognitively and physiologically burdensome. Emotional suppression has been linked to increased experience of negative emotions and depression, impacting one's nervous system and endocrine system and leading to worsened physical health.

> ⚷ **KEY CONCEPT**
>
> *Avoiding introspection impedes enjoyment in the long run and may actually impact your physiology.*

## Spiritual Bypass

Suppression and spiritual bypass are different functions. Spiritual bypass is when we opt for what is sometimes called "toxic positivity", which is prominent in a lot of people these days. It is when someone is on a spiritual path and any kind of negativity or any kind of realness that intrudes into their reality becomes the enemy. Some people misperceive spirituality as being light, fluffy and positive all the time. "I have to be nice all the time, an exemplary human being." Darkness and shadow, as well as light, have a very important place in living a truly spiritual life.

With bypass we end up not doing our inner work. We try in a tricky sort of way to "jack the system." It is not uncommon to see spiritual bypass in people who are very spiritual. They do their meditation and seem very peaceful, but any kind of disruption can be very disturbing for them. Their only go to at that point is to project onto the other as negative and not face the deeper negativity within themselves. That is the bypass, going around "the thing" either within themselves or in the other person and not dealing with it.

This is very common in spiritual circles and is a way to avoid doing the deep inner work. Some do not want to face experiences that are uncomfortable within themselves. It is based in the shadow work that we will discuss more in depth later in this book. The shadow stuff does not match their self-image or identity. If they have a part of themselves that does not align with who they think they are, they will have to shut that out of their consciousness.

It comes down to a lifestyle choice. Once you opt to take on the inner realm, you are going to eventually face some shadow stuff. Bypass, externalization, distraction and suppression are little tricks of the mind that we employ to keep from having to face what is occurring on the inside.

Understanding the methods for avoiding introspection is an important tool in learning to place your attention inward and how valuable the process is. In the next section we will provide you with a powerful method for knowing how and where to best direct your attention when you take your inward glance: inquiry.

## The Method of Inquiry

What is inquiry?

When we talk about inquiry, we are talking about any question or concept that gets us to look within ourselves. Typically, when I am working with someone, I ask questions that direct their own attention deeper within themselves. To get your answers you will be asked questions and then you direct your attention inward.

Once you understand inquiry, you can do this for yourself. The questions do not have to always be verbally specified either. They can be a simple noticing, such as noticing a sensation, which itself is an inquiry. It does not always have to be a direct question. It is directing your own or someone else's attention inward or deeper. Inquiry means your attention is inward—to "in-quire." Inquiry goes along with a lifestyle change and eventually learning to do your own self-inquiries. Here are some self-inquiry types of questions. Consider asking yourself:

▸ What am I actually experiencing here?

▸ How was this particular experience created?

▸ What is going on under the surface that I may not be noticing?

## Exercise

**Take a few moments to do some self-directed inquiry. Scan your body. Notice your breathing. What are you feeling? How is your mind today? Whatever you can notice…explore, get curious!**

Inquiry does not always have to be in the form of a question. As an example: If we say, "Hey, direct your attention to what is going on in your solar plexus right now", that is also inquiry.

This process is along the lines of Vipassana Meditation or self-transformation through self-observation. It is also called insight meditation. The words in-quiry, in-sight, in-trospection, in-ternal, each begin with "in." They specify the direction you are looking—within. Are you noticing within or without? Noticing within is the key to effective inquiry.

As we've discussed, in our society we tend to look outward. We tend to look for others to provide the answer, others to blame or others to support us. We even look outward for joy. For example, we may feel as if we have to be at the beach or to see an amazing sunset in order to feel joy.

Well, the joy is getting created within you.

In this example, we can begin to explore with inquiry. What is actually going on? How are you creating joy? Have you ever asked, "I wonder how I could create that joy even if I am not doing the external activity that usually brings it?"

This can be empowering because you can bring up those feelings yourself by simply doing a little bit of inner work. You can feel that joy and peace of a sunset just by imagining it. The peace and joy of it is happening inside of you!

It may seem an unbelievable concept to some, but it is always available to each of us.

Inquiry can be used in many ways, and we will ask many inquiry questions throughout the book. However, as we mentioned in the Introduction, there are other types of larger life questions that have a bigger impact on each of us. We call these the guiding questions and the first one is the biggest and most challenging for many people.

▲ ▲ ▲

# CHAPTER 5

# The First Guiding Question: It's All About "You"

## First Guiding Question: Who Are You?

This is one of life's biggest questions, and sometimes getting an answer can be a bit daunting. You begin to know yourself better as you age and mature, but the answer might never be something definite. It is a lifelong question, and leads more to of a "way of life." This question challenges everyone, because each of us must go within to answer it and answer it in one's own unique way.

Some of us may not always be fully comfortable or sure of the inner terrain. Yet asking this question can initiate a process for you to discover who you are. As you go deeper, the real answer to this question is the unfolding of your life and your identity. When we use the word "identity", it needs to be more clearly specified. First, let's make a distinction between your spiritual identity and your individual identity. Second, there is the distinction between your authentic individuality and your conditioned identity, what we call the false self.

We will explain the first distinction now and the second one in a later section of this part called "Your True Self/False Self Identities." You may say that your identity is someone who likes books. This is a self-definition, an attempt at some concreteness for who you think you are. The mind wants to have a concrete answer to the question "Who am I?" But in your true identity, you defy definition. You are much more than your own mind can wrap itself around. We call this greater you or your "spiritual identity."

When you ask the question "Who am I?" you might think of your personal identity as who you are. But this identity is a created mental concept of who you are. It is who you think you are, but it is not the whole truth of you. It includes your personality, but there is a much deeper part of you, of all of us. It is your center. The center of your being is not something that can be defined by your mind, and yet this is your true identity. We will guide you to a better understanding of this in Part Three.

It is helpful to not be affixed to who you think you are or think you must be. Are you placing your identity in your personality OR is your identity at your center? As a reminder, your center allows you to create your personal definition of who you are and to have the totality òf your human experiences?

Another important concept is the distinction between who you are (your identity) and what you experience. Your identity does not have to be determined by any of your experiences. That means you are not what you may think, feel or do. What if you are the one experiencing and not what you experience? What does this do for your identity?

Your identity also comes down to your individuality. There is an authentic individuality for each person which is also who you are. It includes the traits you were born with, your incarnation, the life you are living out. You can fully appreciate all aspects of yourself, such as your gifts, your talents, your challenges.

## ⚷ KEY CONCEPT

*Authentic Individuality refers to your gifts, talents, and challenges. Spiritual Identity refers to you in your interconnectedness.*

When you come from your center, you fully accept the uniqueness of yourself and others without judgment. But the center within us also holds our spiritual identity, our place of abundance and our interconnectedness. This is the place where we are all one. When you ask, "Who am I?", consider the paradox of having both an authentic individual identity and an infinite spiritual identity.

One way to approach the spiritual identity is to break the question up and turn it around. We can move from "Who am I?" to "Who I am." "I am" is the same as being; it is simply saying you exist. Thus, one could say who you are is the being existing as "<insert your name>." Then who is that being? That is the part of your experience that must always remain undefined, unbiased and non-judgmental.

It begins to point to the "objective observer" in each of us. There is a part in your mind that notices. The next exercise will help you notice the noticer.

## Exercise

Please take a moment and notice that you have the ability to notice. If your attention begins to wander this is okay; you can notice, only now you are noticing something else. Now take moment and ask yourself, "Who is actually doing this thing called noticing?"

Can you notice that there is a part of you that objectively notices without judging or evaluating the content of what you notice? A part that is completely objective and indifferent to whatever is being noticed. Completely neutral to whatever is being observed...like an eye ("I") that only sees but is not evaluating what it sees...an objective observer.

That is noticing the noticer.

That noticer is generally what we call "I." If we make the phrase, "I love myself", this is where the English language betrays a little bit and exposes something. In that sentence there is "I" and there is "myself." In reality my "I" and self are not separate.

Who is the "I" that is loving? Who is the self that is being loved? There is only one being, and that is you, who you really are.

Though you can notice the noticer, there is much more to your spiritual identity. It is important to know that trying to "figure it out" is not going to work, because that is your mind trying to get around something greater than itself, like a snake trying to swallow a buffalo. We will explore your spiritual identity more throughout the book, but for now let's consider exploring the mind itself. Sometimes the mind gets a bad rap for getting in the way of the spiritual identity. But your mind has its own brilliance as the creator of all you experience in life.

CHAPTER 6

▲ ▲ ▲

# Exploring the Brilliance of Your Mind

## An Introduction to Mind-Body Consciousness

B ody and mind are two sides of the same coin...you. Each of us is a body-mind individual. The mind itself can be classified into conscious and unconscious minds, that which you are aware of and that which you are not. Yet it is really only one mind.

Your mind creates your experiences, every one of them. Most of us are usually unaware of the deeper inner aspects of our experiences. Also, if your mind is actually creating your experiences, how does it do that? How does that actually happen? That goodie will be revealed as we go deeper on our journey.

For now, it is better to understand your mind as the creator of your experiences, of which there are both conscious and unconscious parts or elements.

### ⚷ KEY CONCEPT

*Your mind creates all of your experiences— both conscious and unconscious.*

As we begin, please turn inward while using the tool of inquiry (or introspection), how you experience your world and your relationships is happening within you. You can begin by noticing your experiences themselves.

Every experience has three components to it: physical, emotional and mental. Of the three components each has aspects that can be conscious or unconscious in varying degrees.

Think of each component as a spectrum with different levels of how conscious or unconscious you are of what is actually happening and how it is being created.

Physical:     conscious ———————————— unconscious

Emotional:  conscious ———————————— unconscious

Mental:       conscious ———————————— unconscious

Awareness of the unconscious aspects of your experiences determines how awake you are and how much choice you have. The key is to make the unconscious conscious. All aspects of an experience, both conscious and unconscious, must be seen in order to change an experience. Furthermore, each experience has a unique "pattern" to it. Once you unravel the pattern, you can change it.

You can begin to approach inner transformation on any level of your experiences. Practice noticing inwardly and shining a light into whatever is hidden or unseen.

For someone more body oriented, you can enter in through the body, maybe doing yoga or other physical activities. Maybe you tend to focus more on behaviors. For this type of individual, what is unconscious may open up more into the emotional and mental structures of an experience.

For someone who is more mentally oriented, they may start with thinking or with a conversation, and then it may open into the emotional and body structure for them.

For someone who is emotionally orientated, they need to have their feelings first before they can go deeper.

Once you begin to notice the other parts of your experiences, you can begin to unravel the pattern, like a vortex spiraling down until you find the root. Patterns usually repeat, but with each deeper rotation you get more and more toward resolution.

There is another part of your mind that hinders your noticing and keeps you bound in self-limiting patterns. This is the judging mind. But rather than dwelling on a negative aspect of your mind, let's jump right into the antidote to the judging mind, which is acceptance.

# The Judging Mind and Acceptance

*"The moment that judgement stops through acceptance of
what it is, you are free of the mind. You have made room for
love, for joy, for peace."*
~Eckhart Tolle

The antidote to judgment is acceptance. Acceptance allows the unconscious parts of your experiences to be revealed and to be seen. Inner transformation begins with noticing and accepting; but what are you accepting?

As we define acceptance, it means not judging what is occurring as good or bad, right or wrong. Acceptance does not mean condoning. You could notice a very negative experience and part of the healing of that experience means you first have to accept that it is occurring. This is generally the meaning of acceptance. It is a state of no judgment.

There is a natural judging function in the mind. This judging mind wants to categorize everything. As we do this, we tend to put things in these good vs. bad, right vs. wrong, or this vs. that type of categories. This is not useful. Judgment and categorization do not lead to transformation; they lead to keeping a problem in place.

Acceptance says for example, "I notice I am feeling a certain sensation in my gut." Acceptance means you accept what is occurring. It is more factual, like noticing and accepting that the sun came up today. You can easily accept that the sun came up today because it aligns with what is true.

Another way to explore acceptance is by asking the question "What is true for you?" Are you having a certain experience or are you not? Are you having a certain emotion or are you not? The reason to practice acceptance is because people judge themselves when they have a negative experience. It is common to think that because someone is having this painful experience, that means something is wrong with them and they have to fix themselves. Therein lies a mistake. The proposition is to look and say, "Okay, I am having this experience. Do I accept that I am having it?" If it can be accepted, then you can take the next step toward transforming it.

MARCEY: This may be a different definition of acceptance. The concept of being a neutral observer or noticer
is challenging because for me, my emotions, body and
mind react so quickly that it seems automatic. The "judge"
is first to the party, before my logical mind can start
processing an event or think logically—before I can even
think that acceptance is an option.

MICHAEL: If you are judging immediately, that tends to
keep content out of your awareness. You will say YES to
the good stuff and NO to the bad stuff. The acceptance
is a state of mind to work within.

Let us say I am talking with someone and they say, for the
sake of an example, "I get so angry I could hit them." The
tendency is to think, "Oh my god! What a terrible thing!"

If one actually did the behavior, that is wrong. One does
not want to go around physically hurting people. However, if someone wants to work with the experience, they
need to accept what is occurring along with feelings of
guilt that might come up. They would need to accept all
the aspects of what is happening that would cause them
to say that (resentment, betrayal, justice, revenge, etc.).

If you want to work with something, you will have to
accept that it is happening and not deny it. Have you
heard the phase "Denial is not just a river in Egypt!"
Acceptance is an antidote to judgment and denial.

MARCEY: That is important and I do not think I have
ever heard that before. If I think of it in regards to raising
children: In my case I hate to nag and get on my kid's case.
If I accepted the fact that I nag and am always on their
case, then at least I could better understand it.

MICHAEL: In this case, if you accept that behavior of nagging, then you can shift it more easily. If nagging is being judged as bad, then you have two things to work with—the nagging and the judgment on top of it.

First, you have to see that you do the specific behavior. What are you trying to get? What is it bringing you? You can explore that. Maybe when you do that behavior it leads you to a deep dark negative feeling inside and you do not want to feel that. By not noticing and accepting the behavior, you do not have to feel that feeling.

Acceptance is going to open the door to allowing you to feel the full extent of your experiences. It will uncover hidden emotions and hidden beliefs. These are necessary keys in creating any changes you want in your life. If you do not fully accept what you are working with, then you do not have all of the pieces and lasting transformation is not going to happen.

## An Example of Going Deeper

MICHAEL: Do you accept that you nag sometimes?

MARCEY: Yes.

MICHAEL: What does that behavior do for you?

MARCEY: It gets things done. It gets the kids to do what they committed to do, like schoolwork for example.

MICHAEL: Why is that important?

MARCEY: Because they need to pass their classes, they need to learn and accomplish the things that they committed to do in school.

MICHAEL: Okay, those sound like pretty good outcomes. Are there any other ways you could work toward those outcomes without nagging?

MARCEY: I have tried! I think being a mother of teenagers, I am trying to teach them. I have tried organization and systems so they can learn to keep themselves accountable, so I do not have to be on their case. Neither of the kids like it. In general people do not want to be told what to do or be nagged, but they are not independent enough yet to have a system in place to keep track of their own stuff and get stuff done.

MICHAEL: What if you had rewards and consequences with no nagging? In fact, you completely let them have the results of their choices.

MARCEY: Right, they are natural consequences. It is hard to see your kids fail, but I know it is necessary. That is how they learn, by having the experience with consequences and not by protecting them from that.

MICHAEL: By nagging you are basically programming them. If they take that into adulthood, they are going to attract nagging people in their life, so they can get stuff done; maybe it is with a nagging spouse or nagging friend. That will become their default way because that is what your training is doing - the only way you get results is by a mom nagging. You can be firm, but I think it is also about the energy behind the communication. You could look at your own frustration in the matter. Once you can remove that out of the mix, it will no longer be nagging.

MARCEY: I was going to mention that sometimes it is easier to nag than to enforce consequences.

MICHAEL: That is your own frustration, that they are not behaving the way you want them to and that is about you.

You can accept the judging mind as well, because our minds judge. If you want to practice acceptance, accept that you also judge. By doing this it becomes less of an issue. You will begin to realize that "yes, my mind judges, but it is not running the show." Once you accept that, you can see the deeper truth. "Oh, there is my judging mind. Okay, nice little judging mind. You are trying to keep me safe. How nice." But let's not stop there.

Full acceptance of yourself leads you to your humanity. It embraces the totality of who you are, your gifts and your challenges. Everything about you in your human incarnation is what acceptance is about. It is fully dropping in to who you are, as you are, each and every moment. I remember when I was younger in my 30s, I had a mantra that I worked with. It was…

*I love and accept myself wholly and completely,
as I am, in each moment.*

This is a complete embrace. We want to embrace most of ourselves but there is also that dark area.

Acceptance is a dimension of love. It is a kind of precursor, where you are practicing the journey to a fuller love within yourself. Acceptance involves inclusion. The best model for understanding inclusion and how to work with it is with a parts model.

Each of us is a whole being comprised of parts. Some parts of yourself you may value and other parts you may not. However, if there are any parts you cannot accept in yourself, these become rejected parts. Begin to include any rejected parts of yourself. If parts have been rejected, it is because you do not want to encounter them. But within the state of acceptance, you are able to make that embrace. The key is to be able to say, "here is this rejected part that I embrace."

As an example, before transforming my inner experiences, I had memories of myself as a lonely little child, alone and crying in the corner. As an adult, I did not want to see that because it conflicted with my self-image. Yet acknowledging and embracing the memory became key to being able to transform my past and experience deeper connections and intimacy with others. Maybe for another person they have memories of being cruel to a sibling and have feelings of guilt around acknowledging that. Yet this can be the road to better relationships and to finding a deeper compassion within.

Once you accept a rejected part and include it, then you can work with it. Then you know where the feelings are coming from. If you reject an experience, you do not move toward wholeness. Inclusion dovetails into that. Inclusion could be another word we could use in conjunction with acceptance.

> MARCEY: I have found it hard sometimes to accept or love what is. For example, I have struggled with accepting certain relationships, my own appearance or fluctuating finances. When I am able to accept what is, I feel a shift in my thoughts and feelings, almost as though they are slightly more neutralized or softened.

> MICHAEL: Some people resist this concept because they think if they accept, that means they have to live with everything as it is. That is not truly the meaning of acceptance. It means accepting as more as a starting point rather than an end point. You have to accept where you are starting from, right?

Let us say you want to go on a journey and you know the destination. You also have to know where you are leaving from, right? If you go to purchase a train ticket to New York, you would be asked from where you are starting. To New York from where? "Oh, I do not know! I just want a ticket to New York."

It is easy when you notice the good stuff, though this could also be challenging for some people. But acceptance means including the shadow. It is accepting the negative parts of your experiences that you do not want and tend to fight against. Accepting does not mean something is always going to be a certain way. That is not it. That is faulty thinking.

Acceptance is also about accepting the past. When we can get to a complete acceptance of the facts of our past, then a big chunk of the work is done. When the past no longer becomes a problem—it was only a state of affairs, and you are no longer bound by it—it neutralizes a lot energetically. It takes the emotional charge off of the issue. Can you feel that? It takes the wind out of what might be holding you back.

Please keep practicing acceptance as it will continue to serve you. Having discussed this very important antidote to the judging mind, let's explore a deeper aspect of the mind. This is the introduction to "reality" and how we each create our own.

## Understanding How Your Mind Creates Your Reality

There are the circumstances of your life and then there is how you experience those circumstances on the inside. It is important to understand perception, to understand that the experiences are happening within you. It is almost as if your whole life is being projected from within your brain which is what science tells us is actually happening. No one truly perceives external reality accurately. Each of us is perceiving it as we re-make it internally. Therefore, the world will give you back the reality that you need to live your life.

In an article published by the Wu Tsai Neurosciences Institute at Stanford University, it states that reality is constructed by your brain. "It is important to understand we're not seeing reality", says neuroscientist Patrick Cavanagh, a research professor at Dartmouth College and a senior fellow at Glendon College in Canada. "We're seeing a story that's being created for us."

As an example, let's say someone constantly feels as though people are letting them down. When this occurs, they feel they cannot rely on others and they constantly feel unsupported. What if no one is truly letting them down, but they perceive that this is happening? In order to shift the pattern, they need to look at the inner states which give rise to this perception. The whole experience of "being let down" is happening within, but their mind creates the perception of it happening by others. Is it possible that people and circumstances show up to reinforce the story of always being let down? If the story and experience shifted around this problem, could those same circumstances and people cease to show up? Let's discuss how people create their reality.

## You Are Creating Your Own Reality

This may seem deep, but it is a good entry point in discussing and understanding the mind and how it functions. What is interesting is that your mind creates your reality (aka your experiences). What is more interesting is that if your mind is creating your reality, how is it actually doing it?

The first point is to understand that your mind actually does this. I do not see a lot of people acknowledging this important point. If we are going to talk about awakening, empowerment and transformation, that means understanding that you are creating your responses, and the reality you are living in, based on how your brain processes the information brought to you by your senses. If you feel frustrated, then you are creating that response to a certain situation. You could also feel at ease with it. Both responses are available options.

Let's take an example. When some people get busy and have a lot of things coming at them, they can easily go into "overwhelm." They may be a single task processor, preferring to do one thing at a time. If three things come at once, there are ways to learn to deal with it effectively, but these responses have to be learned.

In the example, if the person is not paying attention, things could come at them and throw them into a state of being overwhelmed. It may seem as though tasks are coming, coming, coming, but it is the person's internal experience of overwhelm that is the problem. In this example, the person could try to control their environment, but that does not work very well.

The key is to understand that the experience is changeable. One does not have to be overwhelmed or be forced to multitask. The first thing is to deal with how the brain is creating the overwhelm. The nuts and bolts of how that happens is in Part Two: Overcoming Your Obstacles.

In our example, once someone feels better on the inside, when several things come at them, more choices are available for their behavior. They can choose not to take something on right now, to postpone it. They can make a list and do it later. Then tasks can be managed in a way that this person does not go into overwhelm. This is best done by first creating a new inner experience to work from—say for instance, ease and flow. They can learn to approach tasks from a calm inner state. As they continue to work with that more and continue changing it, the experience of overwhelm might disappear altogether.

Another option is to become aware of this feeling of overwhelm and not change any of it because being overwhelmed is okay. Some may decide to not challenge the overwhelm anymore and realize, "Okay, this is it. This feels like a consequence of being a single-tasking person in a multitasking world", and that is okay. They can live with it and find ways to work with it. At the core the person continues to be a single-tasking person and that is what feels authentic to them.

But what if there is something else creating the overwhelm? It could be coming from a different place. For instance, if you are constantly overwhelmed in life and it doesn't feel authentic, then you might choose to work on shifting this around. This is an important distinction. When overwhelm does not feel authentic to your natural way of being, then you have the choice to change it.

By understanding what feels authentically you, you may start feeling a sense of empowerment as you honor your natural inclinations. By doing this, by being your own authority on yourself, you will get to know yourself better.

> MARCEY: One area where I used to be self-critical was my ability to stick to things. I would learn how to do something new, do it, then move on to something else. As an example, I had a home-organizing small business for a short time but it never became a career. There were times when I thought about the business and felt defeated about what it could or should have been.

> I later learned that one of my own authentic characteristics is a love of learning. Once I understood that, I felt much better about the variety of books, classes, conferences and studies I have done on different subjects. For me it was about the learning something new and not about the mastery of it or need to turn it into my next life mission. With this understanding I could celebrate my curiosity as part of my authentic self and try new things without expectations.

MICHAEL: That is a great example. It comes down to being your own authority. Let's discuss this a bit more.

## Being Your Own Authority

It is important to know that you are your own authority, the final word. This is about being in charge of the process, even if you are working with someone else, be it a coach, mentor, guide or teacher. Any outside helper should know they are working for you and that you are the ultimate authority. It does not preclude you from seeking advice; you can ask questions and get feedback. Here we are talking about the authority, the final word when it comes to your life choices and decisions. A good manager will gain input from their people and then decide how to proceed based on the input. Sometimes we need to sample the outside world to get different points of view.

However, when you put your authority in someone else's decision, that is where you lose power. You do not need to have all the answers all of the time. Part of being an authority is accepting when you do not know. While you can gain information—do your research and talk with your people—when it comes to the bigger decisions in your life, you are the authority. It is going to come down to you, in the end, making the right choice for yourself.

This means trusting yourself, even if you make a mistake. Know that if you operate from this place of being your own authority, while learning the tools to understand the timeliness and correctness of decisions (more in future chapters), then there are no mistakes. This will help you learn to start leaning into and trusting yourself over other people, and accepting that it is okay to make mistakes.

Instead of mistakes, it is feedback. If you make a mistake, it provides you with feedback for how to proceed. We have to get away from the concept of failure and mistakes as a bad thing. Those are feedback mechanisms to help you hone your inner truth. If you missed the mark, that is okay because the next time you have a better idea of where the mark is. There is a phrase in Neuro Linguistic Programming that they teach in the beginning: "There is no such thing as failure, only feedback."

You need feedback to understand the results of your choices and actions. If you put out a ping into the world and no feedback comes back, you do not genuinely know how it is landing. You have no ways to gauge the effectiveness of what you are doing. This is where some people get a bit nervous, when they want the world to respond positively. It can feel vulnerable, like an artist sharing their work. Am I going to get the response I want? Am I going to be accepted? Is the world going to see what I see in myself?

The world cannot see you as an authority until you first know your own inner authority. We could posit that there are two kinds of authority, an outer authority and an inner one. If you want to show up in the world as an outer authority, you must be in touch with your inner authority. Ask yourself, "How do I know the right choices for myself? Am I making those choices? Am I taking that level of accountability and responsibility for myself and my life path?"

## ⚷ KEY CONCEPT

*The world cannot see you as an authority until you first know your own inner authority.*

Now with your inner authority firmly established, let's dive deeper into consciousness...what it means to be awake and aware. To do this we will need a map or model to help us navigate the inner terrain.

# CHAPTER 7

# Tools for Working with Consciousness

## A Model for Consciousness

A map is not the territory but a representation or a model for the territory it represents.

In this section we will explore a highly useful model for mapping consciousness or the inner terrain. Remember, this is only a map and should be taken as such. The ultimate authority regarding the actual terrain is you. However, once you come to understand the concepts in this model, they will be helpful in your deeper transformative journey.

## Jung's Model for Consciousness

This model is from the work of Carl Jung. It shows three layers to your consciousness: persona, shadow and essence. These may or may not be new terms but we will explain their meaning as we are using them:

**Persona** (image)

↳ **Shadow** (what's hidden)

↳ **Essence** (your being, your true self, who you are)

**Persona** is the mask(s) you wear in the outer world; it is the self-image you project to others and how you wish to be perceived. It is how you reference yourself in terms of the outer reflections the world gives back to you. What happens when you take off the mask? There is more going on behind the facade. What would it be like for you to have the mask and also be able to remove it at will? Some people think you must get rid of your persona, that you have to get to the essence and only be in essence without a persona. But we all have our personas. The persona can be considered as a translation device. It allows you to interface with the world. It is part of your personality; it is part of you but not the whole of you. There is more to you—persona, shadow and essence. The tendency, however, is to get more identified with the persona and miss the greater truth.

**Shadow** is the part of yourself that tends to stay hidden or unconscious. These are things you do not want to see in yourself, your life and your experiences. Much of the time these are unresolved childhood needs and issues that interfere with adult behavior and communication. Examples would include feelings of being unloved, rejected or an internalized shame from being improperly parented. Also included in this category are primal feelings and urges, such as aggression, pleasure and fear. This is where the externalization, repression, distraction and spiritual bypass—those things that we talked about earlier—come into play. Those are methods for not having to look at your shadow.

What typically happens when one does this work is they eventually hit that shadow which does not feel good. It is not what they want, so they go back out and get more invested in the persona, in the image they are trying to create, in this self-image of how people are perceiving them, and what the world is reflecting back to them.

That process begins to create a "false self" or a false self-identity. Remember, having a persona or a shadow is not false. But when you get identified with only your persona, while repressing your shadow and missing entirely the core of who you are, that is when your identity becomes false.

**Essence** is who you really are, your true self. It is what is true about you—your individual essence and spiritual core. It is the qualities that are true about you, the things you have learned and integrated, the things you naturally had from birth. It is that which will always be at your core as well as your core values. It is the center of your loving nature and your love for the important people in your life. It also holds the mystery of your collective connection with others and all that is. Let's say a bit more about this mystery.

When you get deep into your essence, it is possible to have mystical experiences and feel you are connected to everyone and everything. One term for this is a "unitive experience", which is always somewhat difficult to describe. As we've mentioned, we will jump into this more as the book progresses. For now, you can define one aspect of essence as who you really are; it is what is true about you. It is your own loving and accepting nature. It is your uniqueness!

## How Does This Operate in the Real World?

If someone is outside of their center and greeting the world only in their persona, they may seem fine, but underneath it they are not. This is when people sense inauthenticity, especially if one is trying to bolster their own self-image in their interactions. People can see through that. They can see that and the shadow starts to show through because they are trying to keep it at bay.

The more you stay in the persona as a false center the more the shadow begins to threaten you. Once you move to the deeper essence, centered in that place, then the  persona and the shadow are external to your center. They are outside of it, but included as a part of your essence. When you shine your essence through the shadow and through persona, you still have a persona but now it gets lit up by that inner essence, by that inner light. This is the light of your awareness that allows what is hidden to be seen—including the shadow dimensions. It lights it all up. That is where the acceptance comes in because now you are going to start to notice some of that shadow as you let your light shine.

This is going deeper from persona and toward the inner realm. Find and feel your desire to find that center, to want to know who you are and live from that place. However, you have to go through that shadow realm to get there. That shadow realm is generally every-thing from your past that is unprocessed, or still having to be dealt with: it is that which got tucked away for a later time. It is also your pri-mal aggressions, drives, hungers and urges. Coming from your essence helps you work with these challeng-ing aspects of your nature.

Personality is part of who you are but not the totality of who you are. You are a whole and complete

## ⚷ KEY CONCEPT

*Your personality is part of you but not all of who you are.*

being with a unique specific personality. Your personality involves aspects such as your name, your likes and dislikes, hobbies and interests, what you do for work and how you communicate.

Your essence is who you are. For example, I am passionate about inner work. I am here to live this stuff and it is what I have been doing. When I get to work with other people, I am living that purpose in the world. This comes through my personality but always from my essence. My shadow might bring up insecurities around this, so then I would have to deal with those insecurities.

Living this stuff goes back to the earlier concept of living in that state of well-being, where well-being is a verb. This is being who you are, not who people want you to be or what others think your purpose should be. It is where you are living in that state of wellness, living from your essence.

Once you are divested of your identification with the persona, you do not care what other people think anymore. Others are going to see what they want anyway. If they are coming from their own persona, they are going to project their own essence or their own shadow onto you. We will talk more about projection and how that works in a bit. The best kind of relationships are when we are meeting essence to essence.

When you come from your essence and you see others from their essence, it supports them to experience essence in themselves. It is also going to push up everything that is in the way of that, those aspects that block essence from shining through.

It is important to know your essence, to know that you are whole and complete. You are love, you are lovable as you are. **That is essence.**

You have an image of how you project yourself out into the world. You prefer a certain style. You have masks you like to wear. **That is persona.**

In between those two, there is a layer of insecurities and pain from your past, the things you would rather not face. In your essence you are a whole and complete being, but in your shadow you might hold false beliefs about yourself (I'm not worthy, I'm a bad person, I'm not lovable as I am, etc.). You might feel bad about yourself (feelings of shame, guilt, regret, etc.) or act out with bad behavior (angry communication with others, act out of control, substance abuse, etc.). **That is shadow.**

If someone wants to see themselves only in the light and not in their shadow, there is going to be a lot of projection. They are going to be doing a lot of "making it the other person's fault" or trying to live out that image of who they think they are.

If you are in your essence, you can acknowledge shadow without getting pulled off center. If you slip you could say, "I made this mistake today; I accept it and love myself." In practicing this orientation, you become more able to shift to better behavior.

Now that we've laid out a model for consciousness, let's cover some helpful tools in preparation for working with consciousness within the transformational context.

## Linguistic and Language Tools

One of the most powerful tools in working with consciousness is the linguistic toolset. Most of what we will discuss in this section comes from the field of Neuro-Linguistic Programming (NLP). Covering the entire NLP toolset is too broad for this book, but some of these most powerful tools can be quite useful and effective on your journey.

⚷ **KEY DEFINITION**

*NLP comprises models, techniques and strategies to help us understand how the language we use influences the way we think and the results we get!*

*~ The Association for NLP*

Linguistic tools, created around the effective use of language, will help give a reference point for how to enter into consciousness through this form of communication. In your inquiry, when you ask a question, that question is most often structured linguistically. Yes, language has structure. When you understand how to best structure your language, you have a powerful tool to work with yourself and others. Also, the way you structure your language directs the experience of the listener.

When people talk about their experiences, their language often reveals deeper insights by what they say or ask. Language is a medium through which you express your interior life, both to yourself and others. However, sometimes language falls short, especially when you try to describe your most profound experiences in life. The language you use is always an approximation or an abstraction of your actual inner experiences. That approximation also falls a bit short at times and results in miscommunication.

Consider the following model:

If you have two people and they are communicating, at the base each person is having a raw experience. We will get down to the nuts and bolts of raw experience in Part Two. For now, it simply means an experience before they make meaning of it—but then at a second level the brain makes meaning of the raw experience. We have a raw experience, then we have the interpretation of the experience based on the meaning in our mind.

When you communicate, you communicate that meaning to the other person. You are typically not communicating the raw experience, but communicating what the meaning is to you by translating that meaning into language. Then your listener has to take that language, decode that language, make their own meaning of what you said, and then translate that meaning back into their own raw experience.

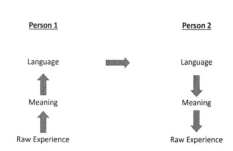

The raw experience goes through multiple transitions and translations over the six different levels, three in one person and three in the other—from raw experience, to meaning and to language in one person to the language, then meaning and then raw experience in the other person. It is phenomenal that we can communicate at all with other people!

The essence of effective communication is when you can step off of your reference points and step into someone else's.

What is your listener actually experiencing deep down? How are they putting their meaning together? What is the preferred language they use?

This is where the linguistic tool can be most useful, in understanding the other person's meaning and eventually getting down to their raw experience.

Much of the time when people speak, they are not aware of the full extent of their experiences. (Recall our discussion earlier about the conscious and unconscious aspect of experience). At the level of language, there are three main tools that keep one from their deeper truth in experiences. These are deletions, distortion, and generalizations—often the sources of miscommunication. By working with these types of speech patterns, it helps you find answers in how you and others are using language, either effectively communicating or not. Understanding these basic patterns helps you recover, clarify and specify information. Below are some simple explanations and examples along with how to use inquiry to shift experiences:

| | |
|---|---|
| **Deletions** Deletions occur when there is missing information in our experiences. For this, we would use inquiry to *recover* any deleted information. | |
| Ex: I don't understand. | Inquiry: What specifically don't you understand? |
| I'm afraid. | Afraid of whom or what? |
| **Distortions** This is when there is inaccurate, skewed or muddled information in what we say. For this, we would use inquiry to *clarify* any distorted information. | |
| Ex: I know they don't like me | Inquiry: How do you know this? |
| Those people are stupid. | Who specifically is stupid about what? |
| **Generalizations** This is when there is inattention to information specificities in one's experience. For this we would use inquiry to *specify* any generalized information | |
| Ex: I always have to work. | Inquiry: Always? Is there ever a time when you didn't? |
| I never get any recognition. | What if you did? What would that be like? |

One of the keys when working with yourself and others is learning linguistic tools to structure language so that your meaning is referenced in the right way.

Here are some examples:

I would never say "Do not worry." I would ask, "What does calm feel like?" It's not useful to tell someone to "calm down". When one hears that when they are not feeling calm, it can anger them, because the worry has not first been respected.

If you know someone is having a bad day, you could say, "Hey, you seem upset right now." You first honor their experience by "pacing" it with them. Pacing means acknowledging what a person is currently experiencing. "I am wondering what it is like for you", and "When you are able to calm down, we can talk it through a little more."

Every word you choose directs the experience of the listener.

Now some might be tempted to call this manipulation. However, every time you communicate it is a form of manipulation because you are choosing the subject for your listener. When your listener is trying to understand you, they have to decode the words you use and that sets a context in their mind. If I ask you about what you had to eat today, at that moment we are not talking about elephants. Yet by reading "elephants", you might now be thinking about elephants!

## A deeper case study example: "Keeping Score"

Sometimes in relationships there could be times when you feel as though you do a lot for another person, and the kindness or thoughtfulness is not reciprocated. It's common to think about the list of what you do for the person versus what they have done for you. This phenomenon could be called "keeping score."

In this example, let us say you want to work with this limiting issue of keeping score. In wanting to get beyond, you may ask, "Why am I keeping score? It doesn't feel good to do it, so why can't I stop? Who would I be without keeping score?"

From a purely linguistic perspective these are not the best questions to ask.

Change the language of the question from "Who would I be without keeping score?" to "Who would I be if giving and receiving help flowed naturally, and what is it like when I can do this?"

The language shift will change your experience as you work with the issue. In shifting the language, you shift the reference point. In the new question there is no longer a reference point for "keeping score" anymore, so you are in a whole new world that your brain will process differently.

## Using "Frames" as a Tool

In NLP there is a term called a "frame"—referring to a frame of reference. If you change the frame (of reference) of something, the meaning will change. This is called a reframe. Reframes are useful to shift your perspective and thus shift your consciousness.

As an example, at the start of the book we talked about you being whole and complete as you are. Nothing is broken, nothing needs to be fixed—this is a reframe.

Reframing something changes how you are looking at it, and in the example above, it is yourself.

Another reframe example is when something negative happens. You start with the concept that things do not happen *to* you, they happen *for* you, and that the seemingly negative experience will eventually have a positive meaning or outcome. Example: You were turned down for a job that you wanted while not knowing that a better job was waiting for you.

As we continue, we will keep adding more tools for working with consciousness and for getting more of the answers you seek.

## The Inquiry Process: Asking the Right Questions

To start "Finding Answers" an important part of your inquiry is learning to ask the right questions. What does that mean? Where could one get started?

Questions create a frame of reference. As an example, if I ask you, "What is the best thing that happened to you in the last week?" You are then going to create a bunch of positive thoughts and feelings for yourself as you pull up the memory. Hopefully, it is going to feel good. Conversely, if I ask you, "What is the worst thing that happened to you last week?" Painful feelings would arise as if something terrible had happened. You might even break down with emotions that are felt in your body.

Questions matter.

It is natural to ask questions such as "Why does this keep happening to me?" or "Why am I going through this?" These why questions take you up into the mind by trying to figure out the answers. This naturally leads to a narrative.

Now narratives are great when you are speaking. It is a gift and can be someone's calling to be able to tell great stories. Furthermore, stories have been important throughout the ages as a way to transmit wisdom from one generation to the next. But it is important to make a distinction here.

The ability to tell a story is different from getting caught in a story of your own making, a story that is most likely not true. When it comes to inner transformation, in creating the changes you want, your story is part of the problem. When you want change, your story keeps you from that change.

It is far more effective to ask questions starting with what or how such as "What is happening?" or "How is this happening?" If you ask, "Why am I in pain?" that question could get you started, but your mind will only spin trying to get the answer. It is not going to get you to shift the pain. Questions such as why can be a distraction, so in that respect it might help you temporarily feel less pain.

> ## 🔑 KEY CONCEPT
>
> *It is more effective to ask what or how questions rather than why because why questions keep the brain forming the story or narrative.*

However, in working to get through the pain there is a better way to go about it.

Instead of asking "Why am I in pain?" consider...

▸ What am I learning?

▸ How am I dealing with my pain?

▸ Can I move beyond this pain and if so, how?

Notice the difference in those two lines of questioning. There may not be immediate answers to the second line of questioning, but it gets you pointed in a different direction, one that tends toward healing and well-being.

The first question—"Why am I in pain?"—is going to loop and loop as your mind tries to problem solve. The second one—"What am I learning?" and "How can I get beyond it?"—shifts how you process it. If I asked you to not think of a purple elephant, you have to think of a purple elephant to try to not think about it. It matters how your mind processes the questions you ask yourself.

Notice how you structure the questions. This is about finding your answers, and you are the only one that can do that. You could look outside yourself, but that is dis-empowering. This is a path of empowerment as you find your own inner answers. That means asking yourself the right question. If you ask a "mentally oriented" question, it is not going to necessarily get the transformative process. In order to go deeper it is essential to ask the right questions, then notice and listen to what comes up when the question is asked.

These have been a few linguistic tools to help you clarify your communication. In the next tool we take a look at desire, the driver for what you want in life.

## Finding the Deeper Desire: What Will Having Your Answers Do for You?

When you desire certain outcomes in your life, it is very important to always explore the deeper desire behind or beyond these outcomes. An effective tool for this exploration is asking the question:

What will having that do for you?

For instance, if someone says they want $100,000 in their bank account, you can explore that desire more deeply by asking, "What will having that do for you?" They may say, "Well, then I'll feel a sense of peace and relaxation." This is what they really want, the peace and relaxation. Before setting goals for the money, they could begin to foster the inner experience of peace and relaxation. It is the inner peace that will eventually lead to the $100,000 in the bank account. Flip it around. This is the power of going for the deeper desire on the inside.

Now let's apply this tool toward finding your own answers. Most of us have legitimate questions. You can get caught up in the mind trying to answer these questions. But when you ask, "What would having my answers do for me" it shows you the deeper desire behind your questions.

Imagine for a moment you got the answers you wanted. What would having your answers do for you?

Would that deeper answer be that you could more easily move forward in your life? Maybe having the answers would bring more peace. However, this could be putting the cart before the horse. Can you move forward before you have your answers or move forward while you are getting your answers? Can you begin to feel a sense of peace as you are getting your answers? The question "What will having your answers do for you?" is a way of getting behind or beyond what you want. There are usually hidden secondary gains for what one wants to experience. It is important to explore and work with the deeper desire.

Here's another example. If you desire a romantic relationship, you can ask yourself what having a great romantic relationship would do for you. The answer may be feeling less lonely or having someone to open up to, to do activities with, to laugh and have fun with.

Would it be possible to find ways to do some of the desired activities for instance, laughing and having fun with others before finding the great romantic relationship, and as a way of attracting one?

Let's continue to add more tools to your toolbox. Again, a reminder: Use a tool if it works; throw it out if it does not.

## The "Current State, Desired State" Tool

When you work with inner transformation there are two states, the current state (what you are currently experiencing) and the desired state (what you want to be experiencing).

When you want to create change, you have to be aware of both states because you are transforming energy from one state into another.

You may have been taught to put your attention only on your vision (desired state), what you want to create, but this avoids looking at what is currently occurring. This is a form of spiritual bypass. It is not paying attention to the status quo, to where you are currently starting from and what needs to change in your current reality.

The flip side is putting your attention only on the status quo (current state) and not creating a reference point for what you want in the desired state. In this approach you may be stuck looping around in the same state. You can spend time decoding, understanding and working on accepting your current state; but if you do not understand your desired state, it is difficult to make progress and change how to function.

If you want to change an experience, you need to work with both states at the same time. Where are you and where you want to be?

The vision, or the desired state, creates the container for where the energy goes, once it transforms from the current state. It is "marked", so your brain knows how to process the changes. You could deconstruct the current state, but that may leave you with nothing to replace it with. When you want to re-engage back into life, to live out your purpose, you need to recreate your experience back into life.

For some of us that happens naturally without having to define it. But for a good portion of us we need a marker, we need some definition of that desired state.

I might ask a client, "What are we working on today?" They will typically tell me, "Oh, I want to create this new thing." Or they will tell me, "Oh, I am stuck in this old thing." They are either going to give me one of the two things, the desired state or the current state.

Transformation always requires both. If you want to take that journey, you need both the departure and the arrival points. Let's take a deeper look at how to best work with your desired state.

The next tool is most useful when you begin to consider the vision for what you want in life. Once you know what you want, the next step is to work with your intentions.

## Forming Powerful Intentions

*"Be mindful of intention. Intention is the seed that creates our future."*
~Jack Kornfield

Any intention you create always originates from your desires, from what you want. It is important and useful to make a distinction between your desires and intentions. Consider **Desire** as the feeling of wanting but not yet having (for instance, wanting more leisure time on your hands). Consider **Intention** as the full experience of what it is like to have your desire fulfilled (what it is like for you if you have more leisure time on your hands). A desire could be to own your dream car, but the intention would be your full experience of being behind the wheel. Of course there is a relationship between the two.

You need desire to tell you what you want and to point you to your intentions. But once you are aware of the desire, the key is to shift into using intentions in order have the full experience.

When you are forming an intention, there are some guidelines that can help the intention be formed in the most useful structure.

First, state your intention in a positive outcome format. For example, if you say that your intention is to "not" have something happen, that is not well-formed. It is more useful to ask, "If I don't want that thing to happen, what is it I do want?" It creates a new reference point.

There are also more questions one could ask in terms of what you want.

**The Meta question**—What would having what you want do for you? (We already covered this.)

**The Ecology questions**—How will this change affect the people in your life? What about other situations? Could this create any new problems as a result of having this change?

It is called "ecology" because it addresses the ecosystem around the change you desire. It considers beforehand the effects of the change to determine if there could be fallout from getting what you want.

Why is it important to consider others when you are setting your own intention?

Let's say there is a husband and wife and the wife wants to be more empowered. She sets the intention and then starts making changes to feel and be more empowered. She gets what she wants, but she does this without considering her ecology. She does not check in with her husband to make sure he is on board with the change. Though she is happy and feels empowered, he feels as if he is not with the same person he married and then he wants out of the marriage. She got what she wanted, but now she has another problem based on not taking her ecology into account upfront. Of course one could say she is better off without him, but had she brought him on board maybe he would have grown as well. One never knows, so it is best to address the ecology up front.

**Chunk size**—Next consider the size of the intention and ask yourself if it is in a good "chunk" size. Consider chunking the intention up or down.

As an example, sometimes people do not accomplish their goal of writing a book because it seems like too big of a project. If you "chunk it down" by only focusing on one part over a certain time period, it may be more manageable. It is making sure that the chunk size or amount of effort and attention is appropriate. Conversely, you might need a bigger intention if the chunk is too small.

**Specificity** - How specific should intentions be? Is more detail better?

Definitely, the more detail the better—the more you step into it. The more you imagine it, the more you get the picture, the feeling, the behaviors that go along with the intention, that detail is what begins to make it well-formed.

Having pictures (as in a vision board) is useful, but it is far more powerful sitting with your intention and feeling what it would be like if you already have it . The feeling inside your body is going to create more power towards creating what you want than looking at a picture or your vision board. Remember, the power is in the "inside/outside" link-up.

Sometimes you have to get in touch with desire, which is the feeling of not having what you want. However, when you move into intention, this is where the shift happens. The feeling is different. Feel what it's like when you imagine having what you want. Imagine it as vividly as possible.

Again, you need desire to point to what you want, but then shift to an intention. Say "This is what my vision is. This is what it is going to feel like when I begin to have it."

### INTENTION EXERCISE

| What would you like to attract, invite, or bring into your life? (a goal, a physical/emotional/pers onality trait, a dream) | |
|---|---|
| What would having this do for you? | How will this change affect the people in your life? |
| What else in your life would be impacted by this change? | Do you need to chunk your intention down into bite-size pieces? Or chunk it up? What does that look like? |

> What would you like to attract, invite, or bring into your life?
>
> Close your eyes and sit quietly with the original desire for the change. What does your inner voice or inner critic say about the change? What else comes up when you think about the change?

Once you begin to hold your intention in your conscious awareness, start to notice if there are any thoughts or feelings that arise which seem counter to your intention. There could be unconscious content that is counter to what you tell yourself you want and the intention might "pull up" this content from your unconscious mind

As you step into your intentions, are they pulling up other things for you to process? If something is holding you back, this can show you what that is.

When you set an intention, there is a "tension" that gets created in terms of what you are intending versus where you are.

Once you set an intention, a lot has to do with where you place your "attention." The intention usually will direct your behavior and attention. A quick way to get a glimpse of your true intention is to look at behavior. Behavior is the best indicator of your true intention.

## ⚷ KEY CONCEPT

*Behavior is the best indicator of your true intention.*

Understanding this will cut to the quick, fast. Many people do not want that much truth that quickly. You can examine your behaviors to check if they are in line with your intentions.

While working on this book, I noticed days when it was difficult to stay engaged. My intention overall was to complete the book. Even though I did not feel like doing the work, I ended up doing it anyway. I asked myself, "How am I doing that?" I realized the intention carried me through (note that I asked myself a how question and not why).

A strong intention can transcend resistance. When you set an intention, if you commit to it, really commit to it, it engages something more. Sometimes providence will kick in and wonderful outcomes occur, which might not have occurred if you did not have the intention.

There are also times to set an intention and then wait before taking action. There is always going to be action involved, of course in terms of your behavior. But sometimes when you set a strong enough intention, if you wait and listen, it may happen by itself. You do not have to "do it" and it happens. All you have to do is have the intention. Sometimes this happens, sometime it requires you own effort.

## An Example by Marcey

**When we go on vacation, before we leave, we will write down our intentions for the vacation. For example, we may write that we want to laugh, relax, meet new people, go on an adventure, etc. We do not describe details, the "how", but instead we set the feelings and tone, then we put the list away. When we stumble on the list later, we notice that we usually experience the majority, if not the whole list of intentions. Instead of micromanaging the time and the tasks, we set the intention as thoughts, energy and feelings. This was definitely a behavior change for this super planner!**

Intention is powerful and it has a different quality than goal setting. When you change it from a noun back into a verb, it becomes the process of *intending.*

When you intend something, you are not attached to it. There is a quality of space around it. There is not a needing it to happen, but more of a willingness to have it happen without necessarily understanding how.

The quality of your intention and how strongly you intend makes the difference. This is not about forcing anything to occur. You can plant seeds, but you cannot force them to grow. Yet with the intention of watering, tilling the soil, and giving the needed support, it helps the garden grow bountiful!

## The Tool of Meditation

*"The quieter you become, the more you are able to hear"*
~Rumi

Before we discuss this topic, let's first let go of any preconceived notions of what you think we are talking about when we use the word meditation. Thinking is part of the problem, and what we are talking about is getting to a state when the mind has calmed down. Too much of the time we think something needs to happen.

But what happens if you sit still long enough without expecting anything to happen? Everything begins to calm down.

How could we use meditation as a tool for working with consciousness?

The primary purpose of meditation is to notice, watch, and understand your mind at deeper and deeper levels, and to observe how your mind works. Think of consciousness as a lake and your thoughts as the surface of the lake. When the surface of the lake (or your everyday mind) is agitated or busy, it is difficult to see down into the depths. When the mind is calm, like when the water is calm, you can see more clearly below the surface.

In meditation you get to a point where you are present in the moment and the mind is slowed or even stopped. Your thinking ceases for a moment. We can call this "being" or the state of "presence." Meditation is the tool of sitting quietly, watching your mind, watching your thought processes, and staying with them in a long enough setting, such that your mind calms down.

Then you notice a state that is calm, but also presence.

It is a tool for the mind to work with the mind. There is a term called the "monkey mind", when your mind hops from topic to topic, which points to how you can get distracted. Remember what we talked about in the introduction: the externalization, the distraction, or looking outside oneself. When you sit in meditation, there is no place to escape to, so you are forced to be with yourself and with the way your mind is informing your reality. The intent is to keep your body still, without moving or fidgeting.

There are many different types of meditation designed to do different things. When we talk about noticing, this is a kind of meditation typically called an insight meditation or Vipassana. There are many different kinds of meditation and it can be a little confusing trying to understand them (e.g., visualization, breathing, Zen, contemplation). For example, there are Tibetan Buddhist meditations in which you visualize very elaborate visualizations for that form of meditation. This is in contrast to Zen meditations where they would call it being more empty or more devoid of content.

In Catholicism there are two types of prayers that are akin to meditations—the Kataphatic (sometimes spelled Cataphatic) prayer and the Apophatic prayer. Kataphatic is when there is content to the prayer. The content could be words, thought or formal prayers. The Apophatic prayer is a content-less prayer. It is being in a state of prayer but there is no dialogue, which is similar to a Zen meditation. It is better referred to as contemplation in the western world. Prayer tends to be more of a form of devotion to the divine, so the intent is different than meditation. For some people meditation and prayer are the culmination of their practice, the end-all, be-all; for others it is a tool in their toolbox. It depends on the individual and their beliefs. For me it can sometimes be both.

For example, I meditated for a lot of years. I would notice my triggers and I would notice when I would react. However, meditation was not the most useful tool for shifting my patterns, once I noticed them. I could catch myself in a pattern and make a choice out of a certain state such as doubt or anger. I was able to have choice on it, but it did not stop it from occurring in the first place. The transformational work I do now came as a result of reaching for a more effective tool. When you can see the pattern, it is still happening. How do you get it to stop altogether? What if it were possible to be completely done with it?

> MARCEY: For me the more I meditate, the faster I notice when I am triggered—almost like retraining or slowing down my mental reaction muscle. I become more conscious of the voices in my head, notice that I handle stress using breathing patterns and reach a deeper state of calm more easily. This seems to make me less reactive to things that trigger me which is a direct byproduct of meditation. It creates a pause button that seems automatic.

> MICHAEL: This is very helpful and we can take it a step further. Which is better—to have a pause on the reaction or not have the reaction at all?

## The Polarity Filters Tool and the Structure of Experience

This next tool is one of my creations and has to do with noticing.

The polarity filter is a tool to help people with noticing. For some people as they begin to look inward, it may be overwhelming. Polarity filters are arbitrarily referenced points that are in opposition to each other. They support noticing more on the physical, energetic, emotional and mental levels within different spectrums.

If you want to notice more depth and detail in what you are experiencing and are having trouble putting a label on it, the polarity filters could help. You could notice and ask, "Am I expanded or contracted in how my body or energy feels?", "Do I feel light or dark in my thinking?", "Am I in despair or joy in my emotional state?", "Or somewhere in between?" Each filter is a spectrum of experiences. Consider the following filters as another way to explore:

### Exploring Patterns with the Polarity Filters

Polarity means 2 'poles' bound together in a union...can't have one without the other!

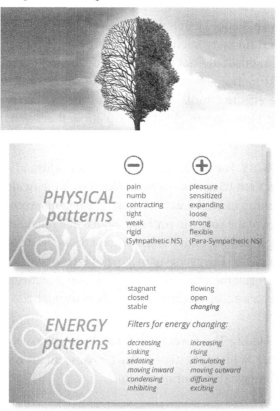

| | ⊖ | ⊕ |
|---|---|---|
| **PHYSICAL** *patterns* | pain | pleasure |
| | numb | sensitized |
| | contracting | expanding |
| | tight | loose |
| | weak | strong |
| | rigid | flexible |
| | (Sympathetic NS) | (Para-Sympathetic NS) |

| | | |
|---|---|---|
| **ENERGY** *patterns* | stagnant | flowing |
| | closed | open |
| | stable | changing |
| | *Filters for energy changing:* | |
| | *decreasing* | *increasing* |
| | *sinking* | *rising* |
| | *sedating* | *stimulating* |
| | *moving inward* | *moving outward* |
| | *condensing* | *diffusing* |
| | *inhibiting* | *exciting* |

| | − | + |
|---|---|---|
| *EMOTIONAL patterns* | despairing<br>repulsed<br>aversion<br>disgust<br>lonely<br>threat | hopeful<br>attracted<br>attachment<br>delight<br>connected<br>*safety—base state* |
| *MENTAL patterns* | negative<br>dark/gloomy<br>judging<br>cloudy<br>agitated<br>denying | positive<br>light/bright<br>discerning<br>clear<br>calm<br>affirming |

These filters go along with pattern recognition and understanding patterns as the structure of our experiences. The tool can help put some language around your patterns. We will discuss patterns and pattern recognition more deeply in Part Two, but for now you can begin to notice patterns with the filters. More specifically, you can use these to increase your acuity in noticing the components that comprise your patterns.

Each pattern has a physical, energetic, emotional and mental component to it; each experience has structure.

If you want to get to real transformation, you must notice the full structure of a particular experience, not only the physical, not only the energy, not only the emotional, not only the mental, but how they come together to form a whole gestalt of a particular experience.

## Client Example

Sometimes I wake up in a "funk", feeling uninspired, drained and not ready to start the day. Mentally, I have a negative attitude and that is what I am aware of. If I looked at each area:

Physically, I feel very heavy, tired, and maybe have some pain in my body.

Emotionally, I feel detached, some despair.

Energetically, I feel stagnant.

Mentally, there is darkness and gloom.

Using this tool helps put language around the areas that are creating this experience of 'funk'. It gives me more definition and characteristics of what is occurring.

Some people might have enough inner acuity that they can tag things. But for a lot of people, this provides an extra lens to look through to make it easier to notice what is happening.

It is helpful to notice what is going on in each of the four places of the filters. If you are a person that notices typically at an emotional level, then maybe you are detached from the physical. Are you also tracking how your energy is feeling?

Can you notice what is going on in the four spaces for any particular experience?

## Structure of Experience Exercise

In a quiet space, identify an experience about which you would like to have more information.

Begin by noticing and labeling what you experience at each of the four levels:

- Physical

- Emotional

- Energetic

- Mental

If you are having challenges with putting labels for each level, use the polarity filters above to assist you in naming what is occurring for you.

If it helps to write down your responses, feel free to do so or capture them in whatever way is right for you.

In the structure of your experiences, there are the components and there is the source, or the space that gives rise to the components and also contains them. The components of experience always arise from this undefined spiritual source, the mystical state. While this is the main topic for Part Three, we need to say a bit about the mystical state as it relates to structure. In any experience there is the physical component, the emotional component, and the mental component, yet they can only exist in the space that allows experience in the first place. This mystical state contains all that is, and yet remains forever undefined and always pregnant with all possibilities. You can think of this state as the great cosmic mother who gives birth to all human experiences. With the understanding of this mystical state as the source of structure, let's focus now on the components themselves.

Imagine an experience like a vortex or spiral. Each of the components form the structure as they work together. Experiences spiral down, layer after layer, culminating in source at its deepest point. The components can also fractalize. You have layers to your experiences. The following picture might help you gain some deeper insights. Consider that the vortex is moving and always creating the experience it represents.

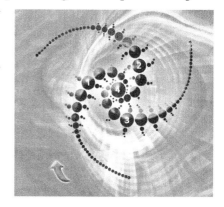

Now we can begin to explore different tools that support transformation. Our first exploration involves a universal theme that affects most of us at one time or another. It will help guide you deeper in your personal empowerment.

CHAPTER 8

## Tools for Transformation

### Power Dynamics: Relinquishing and Re-Establishing Your Inner Power

Here is a classic pattern to help you understand dysfunctional power dynamics—also known as co-dependence.

Take the fairy tale of the damsel, the villain and the hero. The damsel is in distress as she gets kidnapped by the dastardly villain who wishes to inflict harm.

Then in the last second, as she is about to meet her peril at the hands of the villain; the hero rushes in, defeats the villain and saves the damsel from her tormenter.

> ⚷ **KEY DEFINITION**
>
> *Codependency in a relationship is when each person involved is mentally, emotionally, physically and/or spiritually reliant on the other.*
> *~Wendy Rose Gould*

- ▶ The damsel is the victim.
- ▶ The villain is the abuser.
- ▶ The hero is the rescuer.

This is a classic codependence pattern and the role positions when you fall out of your power. The victim, abuser and rescuer triangulate in how they relate. It

is called the Karpman Drama Triangle. Each position needs the others in order to play out their role. It is common in these roles to become identified with the position and then get stuck. Any of these roles can triangulate and bond with the other poles of the triangle. The only way to get out is to re-empower and rise above the whole dynamic.

Remember, everyone is whole and complete as they are; no one needs fixing, no one needs saving. When I am working with others, I continue to affirm this so I do not fall into the rescuer role. This role can sometimes show up even when someone is being of service, and helping others or volunteering. The intention may be "to be of service", yet an inner voice knows the right answer is to not step in, and to learn to say "no." Whether or not this is the case depends on the individual.

## Re-Empowerment

To break away from the triangulation of codependent patterns (e.g., victim, abuser and rescuer) one needs to understand "re-empowerment" or rising above the dynamic.

The question is: How can you re-empower yourself when you notice that you are in one of these roles?

Re-empowerment begins with choice and the locus of choice: Is it inside of you or outside of you? Power always comes down to this—choice and freewill. That is your power—having the ability to choose. If choice is an issue for you, could you choose to choose?

Here is one way to re-empower using linguistic tools: If you say, "You made me feel this way", that is an indication that you are in a codependent pattern. There is an opportunity to shift it around. Some may say it is just semantics, but it is more than that. Re-empowerment comes when you choose to restructure how you view situations and circumstances. The more empowered alternative is "When you did that behavior, I felt this feeling."

> **o⃗ KEY CONCEPT**
>
> *Re-empowerment comes when you choose to restructure how you view situations and circumstances.*

It is the same experience. You are dealing with it, but you no longer make another person the cause of your experience. You are simply sharing that this is what you felt when someone did a certain behavior. You are the cause of it and you are communicating your experience to the other person.

There is another option where communication may not be required. This is when you realize that it is not important and nothing needs to be said. You could go on your way because this situation or person does not warrant your energy or attention. However, if it is someone who matters to you, then you want to be able to communicate with them in an empowered way.

To start, first notice and accept when you get "caught" or "hooked". Most people do not stop to see themselves in these patterns. However, once you notice through this lens, you can say, "Oh, I am actually doing that. I am playing the victim here." Once you can see your involvement in the role, then it is easier to understand that you are not a victim of these circumstances or of the other person.

How does it change if you stop making the other person the cause?

If you are in the victim role, you realize that no one is "doing" anything to you. If you are in the abuser role, you stop your aggressive behavior and communication toward others. If you are in the rescuer role, you no longer look for people to rescue, but see others as capable, whole and complete. In each of the cases, there is most likely deeper work to do once you lose the comfort of the roles—as you go deeper you become more empowered.

Power and choice are closely related. Underneath the codependent patterns are usually feelings of powerlessness. The problem with powerlessness is that one experiences a loss of choice, including over their own behaviors. Reestablishing choice as centered within yourself is the essence of empowerment.

Remember, no one causes you to think, feel or do anything, ever. Imagine what it is like if no one else ever again is the cause of what you think, feel and do.

Of course, there are outer catalysts and other people involved. Living in the world, we are likely to get our buttons pushed every now and then. The empowering difference is that, once a button is pushed, you are able to own that the button is within yourself, and that the reaction is your own part to deal with.

You may be familiar with the concept that "no one can make you feel a certain way, that they are only the trigger", but in the moment it can be very difficult to not react. It takes an understanding of oneself to stop, pause, or step back and identify the behavior.

Stopping is a key concept here—being able to wait or not react immediately. Generally, what should you do if you notice you are triggered? The answer is simple—wait until it passes. If it is something that you need to talk to someone about, then wait. If you try to talk it out while you are reactive, it is only going to exacerbate what is going on. A lot of times these power patterns can come down to attention and our need for it from others.

Everybody wants to be seen; everybody wants attention. A lot of times people will engage in the codependent triangulation because they are trying to get something from other people rather than finding it within themselves. For example, maybe someone wants someone else's attention, wanting to be loved or wanting to feel good about themself. Note that we are rarely aware of these dynamics when they are happening.

There is usually an underlying secondary reason why someone might want to engage the codependent roles, but this unravels itself if you begin to take ownership of the problem. You can ask yourself, "What does it do for me to engage in that? What am I gaining by playing a victim, abuser or rescuer? What am I actually trying to gain here?"

Usually, we want to be loved. These codependent patterns are failed attempts at getting love from our relationships.

Do people lean usually to one role or another, or act in combinations depending on who they are interacting with?

Many people have become very adept at using all three of the roles throughout life, but we tend to have our favorite. Usually, two of the roles will tend to remain hidden. You may see that you are "doing a victim role", but you might not see that you can also play the abuser or the rescuer. That does not mean everyone is always engaging in these roles. Sometimes you might slip into a role on occasion or in certain relationships. Empowered people rarely fall into those patterns, and if they happen to they quickly notice and re-empower.

If something does not feel correct, if there is an inappropriate conflict, usually you can see these patterns playing out. Remember, once you see it then you can begin to work with it.

MARCEY: I could relate to victim and rescuer, but then I think of being a parent. That is probably the closest I have come to being an abuser, when I do the parental nagging or lose patience. How does somebody recognize that they are in that abuser position, and how do you re-empower yourself and rise above that role?

MICHAEL: It is the same. Let's imagine a tetrahedron. The roles are on one side, but there is a point on the other end of it. The one point would be the totally empowered point; the other three points would be the powerless points. The whole thing is on a power spectrum from feeling powerless (I have no choice; I am stuck) to complete empowerment (I am aware of this; I have been creating this; I am empowered and making a new choice).

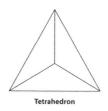

Tetrahedron

The deeper theme is empowering yourself. The roles are like a litmus test, an overlay, a check on any tendency to avoid noticing. Ask, "Am I doing codependent behaviors, either in my actions or communications?" People can also play these roles with themselves internally. Some people split their own consciousness and become abusive and victimizing within themself and toward themself.

For example, let's say you do a behavior that is not in line with your intentions, such as eating a whole chocolate cake. You eat the cake then beat yourself up for it, right? That is abusive. You made a poor choice but on top of that you are punishing yourself for it.

When the punishing occurs, part is the punisher and part is the recipient of the punishment—that is the abuser and the victim, only now they are internalized. Maybe another part rushes in and tries to rescue themself from this inner dilemma. Then they are stuck again. These power dynamics can happen within ourselves as well as in our relationships. When you regain your power, you can make more positive choices for yourself and your relationships.

Now that we have laid out a model along with tools for navigating consciousness, we are ready to use them in a deeper way. We will touch briefly on Abraham Maslow's' hierarchy of needs as another model for human development. Some of you may find it useful to explore this further on your own.

## Maslow's Theory of Self-Actualizing

Maslow talked about a hierarchy of needs. The process that he coined is "self-actualization", to actualize yourself, which we can equate to living your purpose. Underneath that apex there are other levels of needs. Here is Maslow's hierarchy:

## Maslow's Hierarchy of Needs

We are all on the road to self-actualizing whether we realize it or not. It helps to be conscious of that journey. By using Maslow's needs analysis for your life, you can identify areas in the triangle that might need attention. Please remember, this is one of many useful maps, and the map is not the territory. A map is helpful, but the real discovery is your own inner truth. That being said, this particular map is quite accurate in terms of what most people need for finding their satisfaction and success in life.

With these kinds of models there are always different ways you can look at it. I prefer replacing self-actualization with the terms "finding your uniqueness" or getting to your true authentic self. Finding your uniqueness is an aspect of your self-actualization. It also helps you develop self-love, a path to your own loving center as your true nature.

Self-actualization does not mean you have to accomplish extraordinary things in the world. It can simply be getting to a place where you appreciate yourself—as you are. Maybe for someone raising their children is fulfilling. Maybe that is their life mission. Each person knows in their own heart what is true for themself.

Understanding yourself through this self-actualization lens means taking a deeper look, and it goes back to the premise of the Inner Guide. If you're going to go for self-actualization, see where you are with that process by being incredibly honest and compassionate with yourself.

A good litmus test is to look at what is showing up in your life. What is your experience? If you are experiencing things differently than what you want or what you think are your goals, wishes or dreams, then that is a good place to start. Be open to the possibility of something to examine.

 **KEY CONCEPT**

*A powerful practice for self-examination is to look at what is showing up in your life.*

Take a moment to reflect on what is showing up in your life. It may be helpful to journal your answers:

- ▸ What is working?
- ▸ What is not working?
- ▸ Who is showing up in your life?
- ▸ What is the state of your environment?

## Your True Self/False Self Identities

Sometimes when you get your buttons pushed or are feeling provoked, you are trying to protect your self-image even if it is limiting and false. Your identity, in this limited respect, is created in your mind. It is who you think you are. There is who you actually are and then there is who you think you are. This limiting aspect of your identity is part of how you self-define. These explorations are ongoing aspects of working with the first guiding question "Who am I?"

As part of self-definition, sometimes people get identified with issues and challenges in their life.

If an experience becomes a problem, say a negative experience, and it gets equated with your identity, then you must shift who you are—which is basically your whole being. Rather than approaching it that way, it is useful to first dis-identify with your challenge or issue. Essentially, "you" are not the problem.

Let's look at an example. Someone might say because they do not have a lot of money, that they are a weak or undisciplined person. They have made up a false belief about themself. They have made the experience of "not having a lot of money" about their identity.

not having a lot of money = being weak/undisciplined

In this case the person tries to work on being a stronger, more disciplined person. If they have money, they think that is going to prove their strength or discipline. However, they are going to struggle trying to get money because they must change who they are in order to have it. It does not become about having more money; it becomes about trying to prove they are a strong and disciplined person, while unconsciously believing deep down that they are weak.

They have made it about who they think they are and not about the experience of having more money. Having more money never changes who you are.

### Exercise

**Look within yourself now to see if there are any "problems." Have you have made the problem about who you are rather than correcting the problem itself? Take this opportunity to dis-identify with anything that has been bothering you by noticing the difference between you and what you are experiencing.**

Identification with aspects of your experience develops a false-self identity. This contrasts with your true self, your authentic identity. Your false self is a mental creation based on your past and the conditioning forces that affected you along the way. It is an adaptation based on who you thought you had to be in order to survive your upbringing. Think of it more as the mask you thought you had to wear in order to live.

Understanding the difference in your true self vs. false self is an important piece in living from your authentic identity. We will now explore the process of de-conditioning. This could also be called de-constructing your false self.

## Deconstructing and Deconditioning Your False Self

In talking about the false self, a lot of what we struggle with is conditioning. This means you were born authentic, as a unique person. Then on top of that you created layers of a false identity, who you thought you had to be.

This creation is done with the best possible intent, to adapt and do the best with the family and circumstances one is born into. It has been an ongoing process since your birth and it gets further entrenched with socialization as you mature. Who did you have to learn to be to adapt to your upbringing?

> **⚷ KEY DEFINITION**
>
> *Conditioning: The process of training or accustoming a person or animal to behave in a certain way or to accept certain circumstances.*

Over time this process creates a conditioned version of yourself.

If you are going to do the inner work, you must decondition or deconstruct that false identity. Working with this can be tricky because it is an unraveling process or an undoing. Also, there are likely useful behaviors that you learned in your conditioning. These might be useful to retain. Remember you are whole and complete; nothing has to be put in and nothing is missing. However, you do need to revise whatever is not allowing you to see that.

When we say everyone is whole and complete as they are, this is true. However, some people may not yet be able to see that in themselves. Maybe they believe other things that are not true about themselves. To decondition you must practice continuing your inquiry, your inward glance, in order to know more and more each day what is correct for you. You must challenge yourself to look deeper by questioning and exploring what is authentic and true for you.

I hope by now you have a clearer understanding of your true and authentic identity. That being said there might be instances where you need to shift a limiting identity.

## The Challenge with Shifting Identity

Shifting one's identity can be difficult. Much of the time when we feel stuck, it is because we have somehow become identified with an experience, such as when we feel fear, and then erroneously believe that we are a scared person. We then make it about who we are, rather than about what we are experiencing. Once this identification happens shifting the experience becomes more difficult, because now we also have to shift our identity. Many times, we put the cart before the horse. We try to shift our experience in order to shift our identity. But this does not work.

If an experience involves your identity, the brain fights hard to maintain the status quo. When it is identity, it runs through your survival centers in your brain. If you are going to shift your identity, your brain begins to code that as if you are going to die.

Let's say someone wants to experience a bigger bank account and they feel strong fear when they work on it. A good place to start is to think about what getting a bigger bank account has to do with one's identity. If they have made that challenge about who they are, then any change is going to feel like a death within the brain. Obviously, it is not. However, because it now involves changing the identity, in the primal centers of their brain they will unconsciously resist the change, as if their life depended on it.

When you get identified with experiences, the brain believes that you are going to die if you change it. It gets coded mentally as, "I am not going to be me anymore. Who am I going to be?"

Neurologically, each morning your brain recreates knowing who you are. It functions in a way that you do not have to remember to do this. There are mechanisms within the brain when you wake up which allow you to already know who you are. What if these mechanisms were not there? You would have to wake up each morning and figure it out. "Oh my God! I got to figure out who I am today! Again!"

Okay, so how do we get out of this dilemma? Easy. We dis-iden-tify with the experience. You are not what you think, feel, or do (the components of experience). You are the one having the experience. Your true identity is like a blank canvas and a set of paints. The painting is your life experience and it is your creation.

> MARCEY: There was a financial advisor who told me that when people get a financial windfall, such as an inheritance or lottery winning, they will spend it down until a point that they're comfortable with. He would see somebody get $100,000 inheritance, but they have only experienced having $20,000 in their bank account. No matter how hard he would try to help them manage the money, they would spend it until it got down to their comfort amount.

It is like a pendulum swinging—it ends in a place where it feels comfortable. Without inner examination you will always end in a place where you feel comfortable with your identity, your history, your story, your judgment—that is your comfort spot. With inner examination and this awareness, you can get to and beyond that spot. Then you can move forward with a windfall!

## Inner Blueprint

When the pendulum swings too far, it can make people feel so uncomfortable that they would not enjoy what they received, even if it is what they wanted. This reveals the inner blueprint. In the inheritance example above, this person has the blueprint that they can only have $20,000.

The key is reprogramming the thoughts, beliefs and systems that usually come from upbringing. Maybe the person grew up in a house where finances were tight, and suddenly they have plenty of money giving them a brand-new experience. A lot of times the brain codes new experiences as dangerous. If something is brand new for you or basically unknown, you may naturally resist it.

For example, The National Center for Children in Poverty published a study which concluded that individuals who experienced poverty as a child were more likely to be poor as adults (compared to those who were never poor). "Social and economic deprivation during childhood and adolescence can have a lasting effect on individuals, making it difficult for children who grow up in low-income families to escape poverty when they become adults. Because the negative effects of deprivation on human development tend to culminate, individuals with greater exposure to poverty during childhood are likely to have more difficulty escaping poverty as adults."

This is why I have clients first imagine fully what they want because it will start to create the experience for them.

If the experience gets on an "approved list of experiences", somewhere in the back of the brain, then we can have it. As an example, let us say having one million dollars is a goal, but our blueprint is coded to only be comfortable with $20,000. The one-million-dollar goal is not an approved experience, so we will be compelled to behave in a way that does not allow us to have it.

It is not so much the behavior but more the blueprint.

Our next section deals with a very specific subset of people getting identified with their experiences. This is core wounding and how we can form identity around the pain points in each of our lives.

## Pain Points and Core Wounding

It is helpful to understand how different people process psychological wounding and more specifically, the wounding from the past. Part of having unique experiences means that people also have different experiences of how they have been wounded. We call these core wounds "pain points:"

▸ Everyone has different pain points.

▸ Pain points can be experienced in various ways.

▸ Some pain points can be easier to overcome; others require diving in deeper.

Pain points exist mostly in the unconscious mind, in the parts of your experiences that you do not want to look at—although they can surely be conscious as well. Sometimes individuals are aware of their pain points, sometimes not. Painful experiences have deeper structures that can elude awareness, but still operate under the surface of the everyday mind.

Often when someone is wanting to heal, they start to focus inward, but eventually they encounter something painful. When this happens, the tendency is to end the inquiry and resume focus on the external world. However, this leaves those pain points unresolved, in the potential to be triggered, always lying just below the threshold of everyday awareness.

Sometimes as you start to get close to a resolution, you can get very uncomfortable for reasons beyond your conscious mind. This discomfort may be because you are close to a breakthrough. You might be getting down to the root cause of an issue.

Some of the strongest pain points that cause people to flee their interior life are: feelings of emptiness, hopelessness, despair, inferiority, helplessness, terror, rage, hatred, jealousy, etc. These would be the emotional components of the more complex structures. Remember, when thinking about transforming these pain points, you also need to include the mental and physical parts as well.

One of the uses of this book is learning how to navigate and transform your pain points—learning the tools to guide you safely as you turn inward.

## Identity Formed Around Core Wounding

Core wounding could be considered an imprint when a wounding experience impacts you so deeply that an identity is formed around a core wounding. These form the deepest aspects of your false self-identity. The wound is actually an experience, then the identity is the belief formed about yourself based on that experience.

For example, if your parent was abusive toward you, then the abuse is the wound. The identity formed around that wound may be "I am not worth it." The abuse could lead to the creation of a false self.

Core wounding is the pain that goes to your center, and it runs interference on living out your authenticity. The wound will operate as a false center. The wound is never your center. It is peripheral to who you are. The problem is getting identified with the wounding. This is when you falsely believe I am the pain vs. the path that supports resolution which is I feel the pain.

It is very natural for an identity to form around a wound. Yet this is where people get stuck. One client I worked with was in great pain, beat himself up, and was in a horrible negative place when we first started. Part of the biggest problem was that he identified with his past painful experiences.

It is as if one says, "I am that wound" versus "I feel that wound."

When the identity is formed around the core wound, the brain will resist change because it is identified with the experience. Anytime there is an identification with an experience (painful or pleasurable), the brain will naturally resist change because of the primal center in the brain (the fight, flight or freeze response).

This is the part of your brain trying to maintain the status quo in order to maintain your identity.

This is why people end up not making progress or creating lasting change. There is a wound, and a false identity gets formed around that wound. Once that false identity is passed through your primal center, that is when the problem happens. That center says, "If I change the core wounding, I must die." It protects the identity. It does not know the difference between your actual survival and the survival of an imagined identity. It treats it exactly the same way.

🔑 **KEY CONCEPT**

*There are parts of your brain that protect your identity including an undesirable identity formed around a core wound. This is why lasting change may be difficult to make. This function feels threatened.*

If you are identified with a wound, then part of your brain is going to work to protect your identity. Another part of you is saying, "I do not want this pain; it hurts. What is wrong that I cannot figure it out?!" It throws the mind in conflict.

In actuality there is nothing wrong—the pain is a neural pathway; it is the identity that is getting routed through the primal center. Remember, that primal center is saying, "In order to survive and to be stable, I must keep this identity going."

So how do you get around this?

You begin to build in safety. You go back and reprogram the past so your identity can shift in a safe way, so that it does not trigger the brain in a danger mode. You have to keep the inquiry safe.

It is more difficult once an identity is formed around a pain point. Then you are dealing with different neurological functions. Then you are dealing with the part of the brain that is trying to keep you alive. This gets into physiology and will be covered more in-depth in Part Two.

The true-self/false-self model of your identity is very usefulness in moving you to your authenticity. We need to discuss one more very tricky aspect of the mind. This aspect is responsible for much confusion and miscommunication. Let's take a look at projection.

## Understanding Projection of Shadow and Essence

*"Everything that irritates us about others can lead us to an understanding of ourselves."*
~Carl Jung

Projection is a psychological function or a trick of the mind. Initially it starts as a protective mechanism. When you project, you are trying to protect your self-image.

Projection happens when there are aspects, both light and dark, that do not align with your self-image. When this is the case, your mind may opt to employ this powerful mechanism called projection. Your mind uses everything external to you as a screen. The aspects that you are not willing to incorporate

## 🔑 KEY DEFINITION

*Projection refers to unconsciously taking unwanted emotions or traits you don't like about yourself and attributing them to someone else.—Karen R. Koenig, M.Ed, LCSW*

become something outside of yourself. Think of the analogy of your consciousness as a film projector and the others as the screen.

When you go on this journey of finding out more deeply who you are, you will also learn about some negative aspects in your psyche. As an example, if there is something I do not like about myself, and I am not ready to deal with it and incorporate it into my identity, then I may project it. This is a natural function.

Generally, you can get a handle on your projections by the people who push your buttons. Most of the time you are projecting onto them. That is why they are bugging you, because they are representing something you do not want to see in yourself. If someone else becomes the representation for that thing that is bugging you and you are not ready to see it, you might villainize that person. It is a way to push them away. You may find unusually strong reactions against this person.

Examples would be when someone lets you down but it was you who let yourself down; or when you feel as though others do not work as hard as you do but it is really your own inner criticism that you are not working hard enough yourself.

In my own life when I was younger, I had a lot of issues with those I perceived as not bright or stupid. I thought of myself as very smart and quick thinking. These certain people would always get under my skin and I could not figure out why. Why do they bug me so much? What is the problem?

I had to realize I had a not bright part of myself that I was trying to keep hidden. I eventually discovered that I can be very naïve and ignorant, almost child-like. When I finally said, "Yeah, you know what? I can do stupid things once in a while", it stopped being a big deal. This reconnected me to a lost innocence and the joy of being innocent or playing the fool.

Now I have a spectrum of choice. I can behave foolish OR wise or foolish AND wise. Guess what happened? Those people stopped bugging me and generally stopped showing up on my radar. After this inner work when somebody who is foolish shows up, they don't trigger the same reaction. I no longer project onto them. Now I know if someone behaves foolishly, it has nothing to do with me; it is their behavior. I do not have to be around them and they do not bother me. I do not get hooked into them.

You will continue to attract those people to project onto into your life if you are not doing the inner work, if you are not owning these aspects of yourself. In my example, there is this inner experience, the inner fool. I now understand that I can be foolish sometimes. If the fool is sitting inside of me and I am not owning it, then foolish people pushing my buttons are going to start showing up in the outer landscape. They will.

Once you own your projections, you are free to make a new choice. For me, in the previous example, of course I want to be on the wise end of things. However, if I continue make a foolish choice once in a while, it is okay. I am not going to beat myself up. I can gently say to myself, "Oh. There is that fool showing up again." What is the fool asking me to notice?

But projections can run deeper in the psyche.

## From Shadow to Essence Projection

Projection also happens with your essence, your gold—the things that are exceedingly great about you. For example, if you have low self-esteem then you might not see that you are actually good at something. Being good at something will not match your low self-esteem identity, so you project it out. You may notice the other people in the world who are good at doing particular things and you would say, "How come I can't discover my gifts?"

This is projecting your gold on to people. "Look how well that person is doing in life! Oh, my goodness, they got their stuff together." This is still projection, only now you are projecting the positive aspects.

You can project your darkness and you can project your light. When you project, you are seeing the inner in the outer versus owning it inside yourself. When you can take it in, you become bigger, and eventually you can shift your inner world.

In my example, if I do not want to go through life behaving like a fool, then I need to own my inner fool as a shadow. When I own it, I am not controlled by it, but it is sitting there on the inside. There are ways that I can incorporate it, so if I act foolish once in a while, it is not a big deal. It does not reflect on my value or my self-image.

As another example, if someone has exceptional organizational abilities, the shadow might be a chaotic messy person. The shadow of chaos could cause anxiety or frustration when any kind of mess occurs. If they are chaotic and messy at times, they might beat themself up.

Chaos and order will always go hand in hand; they go together. While someone might prefer the order, once in a while they can begin to explore the chaos. Once they say, "Okay, I am making room for chaos and it is ok", then it will not be such a huge problem. They could say, "Oops, I made a mess of things and now I am going to move back to what I prefer, my order, a nice and calm environment." Conversely, for another messy might be comfortable and having order is the shadow. Again it depends on the individual and on their particular orientation.

When you do not own that shadow, that is when you have problems. That is when you beat yourself up or when you have personality conflicts within yourself and with other people. Yet this is not a level of awareness most people want to go to.

> MARCEY: In the example, going from messy and dis-organized to order again and feeling "back on track", between those two points there is a lot of chaos, pro-jection, anger, victimization and blame. Compare this to a different perspective—that the level of organization ebbs and flows. Through this work and in accepting how this naturally ebbs and flows in my life, it has shown me how to live in these two states without being derailed or self-critical.

Other examples:

▸ Productive and the shadow of lazy

▸ Beauty and the shadow of ugly

▸ Kindness and the shadow of mean

▸ Selfless and the shadow of selfish

## Client Example

The client asks about dealing with difficult people: "This shows up in my life when I try to deal with particular people, especially know-it-alls who also demand to be heard. Is the work to be aware that there are also times that I am a know-it-all? I can see how there are times when I tell people things to keep them in line because they do not know what they are doing."

Yes, and take this with grain of salt. This goes deep and for some it is almost too deep, too quick. It can be like taking too much truth serum too fast. If you can, admit that you have done that same thing, maybe not to the same degree, but that you have acted with this same behavior.

That is what the shadow is like.

Maybe there is a person who is an obvious case of this personality trait, or maybe it is more subtle and does not always show up. Realize that there is that element of knowing it all in yourself. When you are okay with your inner "know it all" and love that part of you, it does not have to dictate your behavior. Conversely, when you are no longer bound to the behavior, it becomes easier to embrace your inner know it all.

Then you can say, "Okay, I do not want that shadow controlling the game", but you can see its effect. You can do that or be that way sometimes. When you own it, the other personality will cease to bother you. You can be a "know it all" sometimes. It is not who you are, but rather a behavior trait that you had not liked in yourself. That is what was bugging you about the other person.

I do not like playing the fool but I can certainly behave pretty foolishly sometimes. The more I embrace that the more I am able to live out my wisdom.

It is a high level of awareness to get to. The stuff that is hardest is the stuff that you do not see. In the next section we will work on transforming the shadow. The shadow has energy. It is useful, but you have to know how to work with the energies. I love my inner fool now. It balances my wisdom so I never feel pressure about having the answers anymore. If I have a foolish moment, I can laugh at it and laugh at myself. It is no big deal and it does not affect who I am.

What about when we see others living their best life, both with success and vulnerability?

Remember that when you see people "out there" or those you may think are living their best life, you are looking at them through your own filtering. They are really a reflection of you.

You are seeing something in those people that you might not see in yourself. Maybe it is that you cannot see yourself living your best life, because you believe you are not. Therefore, you have to see the other people out in the world living their best life and then ask yourself why you aren't.

This is the problem with projection. You project out that which is not within your identity structure—it can be good or bad. This is the shadow—that which is hidden. The shadow can hold your wounds and it can also hold your gold.

Why can't you implant new thoughts of greatness and "gold"?

Well, I do not and personally would not. I would not implant anything in; I would try to take it out. If you are trying to implant greatness, why do you need to think you are great? If you're trying to prove or convince yourself, this is a bit suspect. What if getting my dishes done today was an act of greatness?

Many of us want to be out in the world in a bigger way or want to have different experiences. However, sometimes in creating these reference points it is not always effective. It can be a form of bypass which doesn't deal with the current state.

You do not know what others are truly experiencing. You do not know what anyone else is going through. Everyone is living their life. To think that some people are living their best life and some people are not is not useful. While it may be true, what we are pointing to is a change in perception which works better. This eliminates the need for comparisons.

You can also challenge your need to inflate your self-identity. Instead, debunk that need—the need to be great. Once you do this you will more than likely be living out your greatness!

We've laid a strong foundation for what you will need to continue with the transformative aspects of this book. Our next section deals with beliefs, the mental root of your experiences.

## Working with Beliefs and Creating New Experiences

Always at the root of your experiences are the beliefs that lock them in place.

It is important to understand that your beliefs determine what you experience and those experiences in turn reinforce the beliefs that created them. At the root of this dynamic is the original experience(s) that created the belief in the first place. This is called an imprint. It is the most effective access point for inner transformation, the neurological key for getting the change you want.

**KEY CONCEPT**

*Beliefs lead to Experiences
that reinforce Beliefs*

Generally, at the core of an experience there is an "imprint" experience, something from the past. That imprint then forms a belief. Belief and experience are two sides of the same coin. One gives rise to the other, but they will always go in a circular way. What you believe is what you experience, and what you experience is what you believe.

Thus, you can create new experiences by creating new beliefs.

As you deconstruct an old experience, you deconstruct old belief systems too. Belief is not the total cause of the experience but it works in conjunction with your emotions, your sensations and your thoughts. It is part of what creates the whole experience.

Beliefs          Experiences

As you shift an experience, an important part is to uncover any hidden or unconscious beliefs that inform whatever you are going through. Then one might ask, "How do I uncover that? How can I get to that?"

Early experiences tend to form your beliefs about life and self. Beliefs can get formed about how life is or about who you are. Another way to put it is, beliefs can form about what is going on outside or about your identity on the inside.

For example, if you are the type of person who thinks life is dangerous, what types of experiences can you imagine will show up? You may wonder why everyone and maybe life itself feels so dangerous and threatening all the time.

Conversely, if you believe life is inherently safe, it will lead to the experience of life being safe. Whichever way you believe will determine what you experience. Those beliefs can be about self as well. You can believe certain things about yourself that give you a certain experience, but the beliefs may not be true about you.

Sometimes people get identified and believe things about themselves that simply are not true. This is when beliefs about self fall into a category of not being useful. There is nothing wrong with it on a moral level, but if you are believing in a lie, it is not useful in terms of knowing who you are and what you are capable of.

As an example, I could believe that I am not good at organization. As long as I believe that, I have a nice reason to never have to organize. It could be true about me that I am challenged by organization, but that does not mean I cannot learn it. It does not mean I am not an organizer. It does not mean there are no other ways to get organized. However, I do not have to believe a lie about it. I do not have to turn it into an "I" statement. Organization is a behavior; it has nothing to do with who I am.

If we unravel this "I am not organized" belief, the disorganized behavior may have come from something that was imprinted, most likely during an early experience. Let us say someone was raised in a family where it was often chaotic. Because of that experience there was no solid foundation for that child. That particular person might be looking for stability or some consistent foundation, but is used to living in the chaos. The chaos seems normal.

The imprinted belief is that life is chaotic. As long as that belief from that early experience continues to operate unrecognized, under the surface, they are going to struggle to find order because the belief will dictate. Until the belief can be recognized, until it can be identified and reprogrammed, the belief from the early experience is going to continue to re-create the experience of life being chaotic.

Generally, beliefs will operate in a cluster—also called a belief system. It is a set of beliefs that operate together. It is common that there could be several beliefs that were formed from an impactful experience. Consider another example of someone growing up with abusive parents. In this case the person believes that they are not worth it or believe that people are inherently mean. They may have many beliefs from that early experience and the beliefs operate together. They cluster and operate as a whole system. When working with clusters we can change the whole cluster by uncovering the imprinting experiences and its corresponding limiting belief.

In my work I have identified common themes for limiting beliefs that clients want to change. Let's explore some examples of common limiting beliefs.

One of the biggest limitations is in the area of self-worth and self-value. Many people underneath their everyday awareness tend to believe they are not worth it. Then, on the surface they engage in activities that attempt to prove they are worth it.

If you have this belief, you end up trying to prove your worth from a place of believing that you are not worth it. Then you are trying to counter what you are unconsciously believing.

"I am not good enough" is a phrase I hear a lot. "I am not good enough to do or have that particular thing" or "I do not deserve it." If you have this type of belief, you may try to compensate for it and try to prove you are more than good enough. There is a common feeling of too little or too much. You may put your esteem and value in front of your goal. Then the goal and achieving the goal becomes more about proving your own self-worth or self-value. When you make it about self, it is not useful. You are taking an intention (something you want to create in life) and making it about self. Within this dynamic you miss the truth which is you are already of value and you have a choice. Once you take on goals and intentions, remember to not make it about self, but about simply having the outcome you want.

If you choose to allow it, you are already enough to do or have a particular outcome. You can debunk any lies you have come to believe in and understand that you are enough and always deserving as you are. You can understand that whatever was going on in child-hood that caused you to believe the "I do not deserve it" lie would need to be updated. You must update the past with the truth. Then you can know that you are enough—already.

Limiting beliefs and experiences that relate to self are the most tenacious ones, because (as we will get into in later chapters) your brain resists change for a number of reasons when it is about yourself.

> MARCEY: We have talked about when people have goals, then achieve them (such as a wealth goal), sometimes achieving the goal does not bring the satisfaction one expected.

> MICHAEL: It is the same feelings of lack of self-worth that are looming under that. No amount of money will change that until you go directly to the self-worth, to your worth, your value, and then change that.

You can begin to debunk beliefs. There are ways through a specific type of questioning to counter limiting beliefs. Suppose someone says, "I am not worth it." I could counter that with a good debunking question, for instance, "What if you were worth it; what would that be like?" or "How would you know if that was not true?" If you answer these types of questions, you have to create a new belief and a new experience.

People can get stuck in some very painful stuff that is rooted in limiting beliefs. For example, there was a client who grew up with an abusive mother. Underneath that is a lot of internalized shame. That is where "I am not good enough" could come from. Sometimes it is worse than not good enough; in some people's cases it is "I am bad or wrong as I am."

In this case a person with this belief may go out in life doing a lot of activities to prove their goodness. They have to try very hard to have good experiences. They have to keep hidden the "I am bad" part which is shame—a toxic hidden shame. They have to keep it hidden because, if they felt it, it would feel horrible. Generally, people repress bad feelings and compensate on the surface.

The alternative is to go in and change the "I am bad" belief about self to another one, such as "my goodness is assured from birth. I am inherently good by nature." Within that context there would be nothing to prove anymore. Imagine the experience if you never had to prove your worth to anyone ever again!

Another example is someone who believes that they are alone. If somebody believes that, they may think or say, "There is nobody there for me. I am and will be alone in life." They are going to constantly be having that running in the background of their consciousness. To shift this, you would have to get in and uncover how that belief was imprinted specifically to you. If you have this belief, you could reprogram the pattern and say, "I am connected. I belong and I am a part of greater systems. I am connected to people and I am worthy of love."

What if someone believes life is drudgery? What do you think their experience is going to be? Probably pretty tiring. One could start by going back and unpacking that belief. That might have been what mom and dad were experiencing, drudgery. So that is what they think about the way life is. That was the example that was set. While the person tries to get on with life, that belief continues to operate under the surface. Then they wonder why they are often so tired.

Here is an example of challenging a belief. I worked with a client who had a belief that you could not have the "mountaintop spirit" in day-to-day life and be successful. There was a simple question I asked in response to this belief. What if you could? What would your life be like?

Consider challenging some of your own limiting beliefs with this type of questioning.

When working with beliefs and experiences, it is not so much the conscious belief but instead the unconscious belief that needs attention.

Understand that sometimes you are unconsciously believing things that you are not consciously aware of.

Hidden beliefs operate under the surface, in the unconscious mind. They lie below the threshold of awareness and are always in operation. Part of the work, if you want deeper transformation, is to uncover those beliefs in service of revising them. It is not useful to uncover them and then do nothing about them. You can change the belief altogether by creating new experiences for yourself.

It usually involves digging deeper to get to those beliefs, especially the hidden ones. You need to unpack what is going on under the surface.

Sometimes it will come out in a phrase and can almost be shocking when you recognize the inner dialogue that accompanies the belief. For example, you might hear yourself say, "I never get what I want". You were probably not aware that you were believing it. We typically only experience the effects of it, but rarely notice the belief itself. There are beliefs around money, around relationships, around self and around life which can be limiting or supportive.

## Create New Experiences–You Have It in You!

Remember what we just learned about beliefs and experience—that your beliefs create your experiences and your experience create your beliefs. Essentially, when you create new experiences, you create new beliefs and vice versa.

The experience itself is going to have three components to it. Remember, every experience is going to have a mental, emotional, physical aspect that could be rooted in a belief. The belief is part of the mental structure, so we include it into the mental part.

If you want to create a new experience, what do you have to believe is true? What are the feelings that go along with that? What are the particular behaviors and sensations in your body that you would be having when you are having this new experience?

Earlier we talked about deconstructing or deconditioning. If you can deconstruct something in the neural processing, then how do we reconstruct a new experience?

The first step is to visualize an image of yourself having what you want. You must create a picture in your mind. This is mental and is done through the imagination. You can think of imagine as "image-in." You are having an internal image in your mind's eye. What are you imagining? Also in your imagination explore the other aspects of your new experience. What is the picture you are looking at in your mind? What is the new belief that supports this picture? What is the emotional component? What is the physical? What are the behaviors you are doing?

Imagine being fully in the experience you want. Imagine what it is like when you have what you want. When you can do this, you have started to create the experience.

When you set that image, your brain begins to process through that point. This leads to certain feelings which give rise to certain behaviors out into the world. You have to imagine it before it can become real.

In referring to the polarity filters you can start working with the four aspects of creating a new pattern. Ask yourself:

▸ What would my mental state be in this new experience?

▸ What would my physical state feel like?

▸ How is my energy level?

▸ What emotions would I experience in this new place?

By doing this you are training yourself to have the experience. People think they need external circumstances to show up before they have the experience. Actually, it is the other way around. When you have the experience internally, this leads to the outer circumstances you want to experience.

As an example, I could have the intention to be in a fancy new house and think that I cannot feel what it feels like to be in the fancy new house, but that is not true. I can imagine and create the experience now in my current living situation of being in the fancy new house.

**🔑 KEY CONCEPT**

*Visualization alone will not shift your external experiences if you do not address the internal limiting beliefs associated with getting what you want.*

It is more than sticking a picture on a vision board. It is almost like inhaling the new experience, bringing it internally into your DNA, versus wishing for it externally. Sometimes with vision boards you look at the fancy new house, but there remains a hidden internal belief that you do not deserve it or that you are not going to get it.

This work gives you the tools to notice and transform any limiting beliefs.

If the internal "I do not deserve it" thought comes up, you can ask, "What is that about?" You can do some inner work to revise the belief and then go back to the new image and the experience that you want. You may have to do that a couple times, because each time a layer of content in resistance to that might come up. Also if you find yourself saying, "I deserve it", this could be an indication that unconsciously you believe you don't. It's not about deserving it; it's about having it.

In my earlier example, if I tell myself, "My little current house sucks! It is so small and the walls are so tight", this is going down the wrong road. Here is an alternative. "I feel what it feels like when I am sitting on my balcony watching my sunset. It is peaceful and spacious." It is a choice to experience that now.

 When you do this, you are creating a new experience for yourself. You have to grow the antennae for what you want to experience. The antennae are your neural pathways and the interconnection of those pathways.

You cannot have an experience until you first have the neural pathway for a particular experience.

Once you put the experience first and say, "Okay, this is what it feels like" and you imagine fully being in your new experience, then it becomes more of a reality. This is the magic.

MARCEY: I have heard before that people may wish for more money. But what they are essentially wishing for is not necessarily the currency, but what that currency will bring to them, such as freedom from financial pressure and the ability to buy a fancy new house if they want. By thinking about what you want to experience internally, then by imagining and integrating that, it seems that you start focusing less on the bank account balance or the square footage of the fancy new house, but on what you truly are yearning for.

In this chapter we talked about current state and desired state. This is very important because when you specify both you can consciously create new experiences. The eventual goal is to make the desired state the present state.

However, when you go through that process, much of the time it is going to pull up hidden layers of the current state. Then you have to do the work of revising those layers. You have to process through the layers until you are able to step into the new experience and live it out. There are behaviors and actions you will have to take, but the feeling is from a new experience. You are doing it from a different inner place, thus the results show up more easily.

To summarize, creating a new experience has to do with defining your desired state, stepping into it, and living it. During this process one of two things can happen. When you step into your desired state, you are either going to experience it and go "Yeah, this is great. It feels wonderful. This is what I want", or you are going to experience whatever is getting in the way of that. Either way it is an opportunity to continue working with what you want.

# CHAPTER 9

▲ ▲ ▲

# Deeper Down the Rabbit Hole

We have now laid out a model for consciousness and how to navigate through a transformational process. Now we want to go deeper. We want to begin to probe the structures of the mind that relate to your physicality. In doing that you will also begin to encounter some shadow aspects. Remember, the shadow is the parts of your internal experiences that you do not want to look at.

We are going to go deeper down the rabbit hole. We call it the rabbit hole because things get less sure. It is a process of unraveling and it is a way of living. Deeper down the rabbit hole means that the mind starts to get out of its comfort zone—the mind might begin to feel confused by not knowing what is going on.

This can be a useful state to get you to deeper aspects of your experiences, the physiology and the "sense" data. These aspects are what we are going to explore when we discuss obstacles and how they get created neurologically inside our brains.

Here is a question. What if someone asks, "After reading Part One, I feel really good. I am setting intentions, understanding how my mind works, and I start to see the outside world a little differently. Isn't this enough?"

Stopping here means you are not going to get a more complete transformation; you are not going to get to the root of what causes a pattern or an experience. You can convince your mind of anything.

Mentally, you have the power to override the deeper aspects of your experience. If you are going to practice transformation, you must get to the root of how your brain is creating these experiences. You need to go deeper. You can stop at any point because this work is always optional. However, to get to those deeper structures, to get to the real transformative pieces, it is going to come down to how your brain is processing information.

## Let's recap the key concepts from Part One:

- ▶ Mountaintop clarity is available in everyday life.

- ▶ Our external experiences are a reflection of what is happening within us.

- ▶ Avoiding introspection impedes enjoyment in the long run and may actually impact your physiology.

- ▶ Authentic Individuality refers to your gifts, talents and challenges. Spiritual Identity refers to you as part of our interconnectedness.

- ▶ Your mind creates all of your experiences—both conscious and unconscious.

- ▶ The world cannot see you as an authority until you first know your own inner authority.

- ▶ Your personality is part of you but not all of who you are.

- ▶ It is more effective to ask what or how questions rather than why because why questions keep the brain forming the story or narrative.

- ▶ Behavior is the best indicator of your true intention.

- ▶ Re-empowerment comes when you choose to restructure how you view situations and circumstances.

- ▶ A powerful practice for self-examination is to look at what is showing up in your life.

- ▶ There are parts of your brain that protect your identity including an undesirable identity formed around a core wound. This is why lasting change can be difficult to make. This function feels threatened.

- ▶ Beliefs lead to Experiences that reinforce Beliefs.

- ▶ Hidden beliefs operate under the surface, beyond your awareness.

- ▶ Visualization alone will not shift your external experiences if you do not address the internal limiting beliefs associated with getting what you want.

Now let's keep going. Welcome to Part Two!

Part Two

# OVERCOMING
# OBSTACLES

# CHAPTER 10

▲ ▲ ▲

# The Second Guiding Question: Exploring Body Consciousness

## Second Guiding Question—What are you?

The guiding question for this section is meant to bring more focus to your body. The first guiding question was "Who are you?" That was about your identity and getting through the mental aspect of your consciousness.

Now we are asking "What are you?" This is about your physiology and functioning as a human being. In that vein we are asking, "What are you?" and by extension, "How do you function best?"

This question is about noticing differences in physiology and beginning to notice that there are things you uniquely need that might be different from things I need at the physiological (or body) level. Everyone has an identity. Everyone has these constructs, but when it comes to our body each body has different needs.

The intent of this question is an ongoing inquiry into how you function best at an organismic level. It can be related to eating the right foods, the right amount of exercise, the right amount of rest, the things that are physiological and within your control to optimize. These will be different for everyone.

This approach is comparable to the lines of Ayurveda (the nutritional arm of yoga) of getting people "typed" in how they function best. There are certain foods I avoid because they are not good for my constitution. You have to look at your own constitution. You cannot change your base constitution the way you can change your mind about something, but you can notice what works and what is the best fuel to put in the engine.

This is a starting point for listening to your body wisdom and understanding your constitution. But this is also a starting point for

## ⚷ KEY CONCEPT

*The limbic system is the part of the brain involved in our behavioral and emotional responses, especially when it comes to behaviors we need for survival: feeding, reproduction and caring for our young, and fight or flight responses.*
*~Univ. of Queensland*

working with how your brain and physical organs function—your limbic system.

When we ask the question "What are you?" one of the first things to understand is the limbic system and its drive for safety and survival.

## Safety and the Fight-Flight-Freeze Response

There is a function in your brain that is the fight-flight-freeze function. Its primary function is to keep you alive. Its job in your brain is to keep the organism—you—alive and safe. That is it.

This part of your brain does not do logic. It does not do rational thinking. It only does safety and threat. In terms of keeping you alive anything that would threaten your life creates a strong reaction at this level of your brain and the reactions are limited to: fight (aggression), flight (withdrawal) or freeze (paralysis).

There is also the link to identity and how this system operates. Remember from Part One that if you are trying to somehow protect an identity, the brain will create the same limbic system reaction as if there is an actual physical threat.

For example, if someone insults another by calling them stupid, and the other person has the identity of a very intelligent person, the comment can be coded in the person's brain the same way as an actual threat to the physical body. The one getting insulted might have a strong reaction, but it is not because of the insult. It is because of their identity as an intelligent person. The insult threatens their identity and the brain reacts as though it were a physical threat, even though nothing physically is being threatened.

As you know you do not have to remember to stay alive. There are parts of your brain that are doing this for you 24/7. If you drill down in consciousness to the levels of your existence that human beings do not normally operate at, you come to this fight-or-flight sensory level, or animal part of your existence. You are human, but you are also animal and animals process things mostly on a sensory level.

In order to work with and get beyond your fight-flight-freeze response, it is important to experience safety. When you feel safe it allows the deeper structures of an experience to be brought to conscious awareness. This part of your brain acts as a gatekeeper. It either shields up from a threat or shields down when you feel safe. Once you feel safe it opens the door to a deeper level, to your feelings.

## Your Body Allows You to Feel

If you did not have your body you would not have the ability to have experiences. More specifically, your body is exceedingly important for the feeling aspect of your experiences. Your feelings

### 🔑 KEY DEFINITION

*Somatic: Relating to the body, especially as distinct from the mind.*

are a very important piece in the field of transformation as well as for your inner guidance. Noticing feelings is an ability that comes easier for some and takes practice for others.

The deeper truth of your experiences comes from the somatic or body level. An experience from the somatic level will often show you more than you could uncover through a verbal inquiry from a mental place. It can show you more quickly and more efficiently if you're willing to see it.

You can begin to explore sensations and your different experiences from a somatic perspective by asking yourself, for example, "Where am I feeling this sensation? What does it feel like in my gut? What do my hips feel like?"

You could go piece by piece through your body and begin to notice experiences at the body level. When there is a particular experience there is a way to start exploring sensations:

## Exercise

Sit still. Keep your spine straight.

Then notice.

What sensations come up? What do you do with those?

Accept them by allowing them to be.

These are the first two levels in working with a somatic approach in transformation. Notice the sensation and allow it.

Sometimes this exercise will begin to unlock some of the emotions that go along with an experience. If you sit quietly long enough and do not try to "wiggle out" of something, generally, the deeper content starts to arise.

Sometimes you can be carrying emotions in your body and you do not notice it until you sit in silence. You may start to recognize a particular feeling or that something was going on that you were not in touch with. That is part of meditation; that is part of noticing.

However, there are instances when noticing and accepting does not get to the desired change in a deeper pattern. In those cases, we need to practice transformation, and that is what this part of the book is about, the deeper keys to transforming your experiences.

For now, this is about noticing the feelings in your body. Recognizing feelings pulls you out of your mind because you actually notice what is happening in your body. It bears repeating: If you did not have your body, you would not have the ability to have experiences. Through this practice of noticing you create an opening for more information. Exploring through your body is the key. Again, your body is very important.

## Deeper Aspects of Your Body

Since the body is what allows you to have experiences, you can begin to build your ability to notice your sensations with finer and finer levels of detail. You might have a sensation, but there are the gross and the subtle levels of the sensations you encounter. Typically, people only notice what is coarse or heavier, but as you progress, you build your acuity to notice the sensations with more and more granularity.

### ☞ KEY CONCEPT

*Without our bodies we would not have experiences. Through the practice of noticing how our bodies respond to the external world, we create a new level of understanding ourselves.*

As things get deeper, as you progress more into the spiritual aspects, or the unknown dimensions of the inner terrain, a lot of times very subtle sensations can have a very big impact. Generally, when the sensations are subtle, they are more difficult to notice. In addition to the awareness of the sensation, as we have mentioned, the location in your body of the various sensations is also a big factor in developing your acuity.

What are you feeling for a certain experience in your body and where are you feeling it?

The body holds certain aspects from many of the experiences in our past. We hold things in our hips, we hold things in our backs, we hold things in our shoulders, and so on. As you start to explore through the body, you can notice where you are holding tension. What happens as you begin to work with that tension (exercise given below)? What content thoughts, feelings, memories or emotions arise as you release certain tensions in your body? This tension is sometimes referred to as our "body armoring." It is a way people protect themselves from the unconscious content they don't want to see.

## Exercise

Gently contract your muscles in a place where you feel tension in your body. What movements make it worse or tighter?

Hold the contraction for a few seconds but only up to the edge of any pain (be mindful of what is appropriate for you and always take care of yourself). Then release.

Notice the sensation of release. Now stretch and expand the opposite way of the contraction. Stretch the exact opposite of the contraction using all the dimensions of the space around and within you. Stretch for a few seconds and then take a rest.

Notice any sensations.

Now repeat the process, this time using more of your whole body included in your contraction and expansion.

Repeat as much as you want in a gentle back and forth manner. Contract, release, expand, rest; contract, release, expand, rest; etc. Be aware of the threshold of any pain. Explore the edges but do NOT force yourself into any pain.

Be mindful of your breath throughout your exploration. Notice any other content (imagery, memories, emotions, thoughts, etc.) that arises in your consciousness as you do this exercise.

What is your experience? How does your body feel? What thoughts came up?

MARCEY: Are you talking about a physical sensation or is it more an emotional feeling? If I ask myself where I feel something and it is in my heart, I may not feel tightness in my chest, but I may feel emotions that hit my heart area. Is there a difference between physical feelings versus emotional thoughts about parts of your body?

MICHAEL: When you are working with transformation, a physical sensation will often have an emotional component to it. If you are aware of the emotional component, that is great; then maybe you can notice some of the physical sensations that go along with it. Sometimes you notice the physical sensations and as you do that, it opens up into emotional content. It could be emotional content that has been repressed in the body.

Be aware that thoughts about your body are different. It is not a body judgment such as, "I do not like my legs." That is different—where you need to practice acceptance of your body.

What we are talking about is where patterns, obstacles and challenges you are working out get held in the body and the transformation of those experiences. For some this may be the first time you have heard that patterns, obstacles and challenges have a connection to your physical body. Studies show that "ever since people's responses to overwhelming experiences have been systematically explored, researchers have noted that a trauma is stored in somatic memory and expressed as changes in the biological stress response" - NIH article "The body keeps the score: memory and the evolving psychobiology of posttraumatic stress".

Everyone has their own body to explore. This is true for everyone regardless of your beliefs. People must first be guided to where they are safe and comfortable, and then it is easier to direct the attention to the deeper parts of experiences.

Your body has this intelligence and these sensations have a story to tell or it may have a message for you. Could you start listening to what sensations are telling you? What is it opening up? Is there something going on there for you?

This is the approach of the experiential way.

# CHAPTER 11

▲ ▲ ▲

# The Body as Your Guide

## The Experiential Way via Body Intelligence

The experiential way means that you reference your reality from the body perspective and from your bodily experiences.

There are aspects of your existence that are not experienced as mental (mind) structures but are experienced in your body. Your physiology and your neurology work together. They determine your biochemistry. The body is fascinating and does a lot below the threshold of your awareness.

What if you could begin to slow your thoughts down enough in order to bring your awareness deeper—to see more of what is happening under the surface of your everyday mind? This is what it means to include or consider the body. You need the body in the experiential way to say what is and is not true for you, to tell you what is a "yes" and what is a "no." Your body becomes your guide.

What are inquires for the experiential way? Here are a few:

▹ How do your thoughts land in your body?

▹ What is the actual felt experience of different people, places, events and environments?

▹ What is the sensation?

▹ What does your energy (sometimes also called chi, prana or life force) do in a particular experience?

For example, you might recognize that your mood and energy depend on the amount and quality of sleep you get. When you recognize this in your body, it is about first getting your physical energy feeling better. When you are feeling better, it leads to your mind operating more clearly.

Have you heard the phrase "mind over matter"? That is the thought that you can control your body by changing your mind. While this is possible, it also overrides your body consciousness.

Remember, your body has its own intelligence and the mind has been in a place of dominance over that intelligence. What would happen if we could flip that around? What if you could say to yourself, "Okay, I am going, through meditation or stillness, to make my mind pliable and soft enough to follow my body"?

For a moment I am going to let my body lead. You will find that the body knows things.

The mind wants to be in charge and thinks it knows, but the body knows pretty instantly. If you begin to listen and reference your experiences through the body, it is a fast-track route. You will begin to notice more in a shorter amount of time.

For example, I could meet a person and suddenly, without them saying a thing, my Solar Plexus is doing backflips and for some unknown reason it does not feel safe. What is going on? I may not understand what is going on, but something in my body is sending warning signs. For me I do not have to fully understand what it is about. Instead, I can trust my body. What you will find is the body always knows and is always correct. It is the mind that gets in the way.

> MARCEY: This is such a different thought. Society sometimes treats us as if our bodies are just objects and can tie worth or value to the physique. We might be tempted to ask questions such as: What do you look like? How fast are you? How tall are you? How beautiful are you? These kinds of questions can lead us astray. Our bodies are unique, wise, and intelligent far beyond measurement, numbers, or likeability/attractiveness.

> MICHAEL: One time I had this imagination that I stepped into my body on a whole other level and imagined it like a sophisticated spaceship, flying through space by

self-functioning controls and switches which were beyond my understanding. My body as this ship could do amazing things, beyond what I thought possible. It was interesting to inhabit it in this way, to get inside and feel as if you are in a very sophisticated vehicle. You are in it right now and it is moving through space. It already knows the way to go, and it is guiding you to success and satisfaction, if you will listen. What would happen if you could be a happy passenger?

It seems radical, but this flips around our understanding. We are not flipping it to body dominance over mind; we are saying that it is time for the mind to follow. The mind has been in charge for around 20,000 years in our human evolution. It has been developing the strategic dominance of mind over matter, but this is no longer working. It is not useful for moving forward in our modern world especially as it gets more and more complex.

What we are suggesting is a navigation system that guides you through the complexity without having to figure it out. The practice is to follow your body because it knows better than your mind. The mind can be deluded much of the time. If you follow your body, it guides you to the people, places and events that are correct for you.

## 🗝 KEY CONCEPT

*When you can begin to listen to the intelligence of your body, it will lead you to people, places and events that are correct for you.*

Remember, you would not be able to have experiences without your body. You cannot truly experience anything without it. You are existing on multiple planes. The body is you on the physical plane.

Your body is your translation device that allows your spirit to be here fully.

One way to explore your body deeper is by looking at structure and energy, aspects of your deeper body wisdom.

## Your Body Has Structure and Energy

Everything has energy. The structure within a form determines how energy flows which in turn determines how well a form functions.

These aspects are important when noticing the body and the more subtle dimensions of your experiences. As you notice energy (and here if needed, you could use the Polarity Filters tool from Part 1), you are building the acuity to notice how your energy operates in your body.

Where it is flowing and where it is not? Typically, where energy does not flow is where we feel pain. There can be congestion (or deficiency) in the flowing of energy at various places throughout our bodies.

Can you simply play with exploring the flow of energy?

> MARCEY: Could you talk more about energy? Because the concept can be confusing.

> MICHAEL: The energy we are talking about is your life force and it goes by a lot of names. They call it Prana in yoga, and Chi in Tai Chi or Qigong. It is Ki in the Japanese traditions. In the West we would call it your lifeforce or your vitality. In the mystery traditions of the West it is your etheric body. In Christianity it might be considered the Holy Spirit.

You have energy; you have life. That energy wants to flow through you. Matter is actually energy. If you broke it down, in reality (and physics has taught us this) there is no such thing as solid matter. It is energy vibrating at different rates that give the appearance of solidness.

Your body is the same way. It is energy vibrating at different rates. But one thing about the body is that you can experience this energy directly when you direct your attention to your lifeforce, mostly centered in the sacral or pelvic area. Your vitality, your sexuality, your motor.

What does your own energy feel like to you? How is that energy flowing in the body? Can you let it flow without blocking it? You use your energy, but do you know the sensations of energy in your body?

In my own experience and as I did more and more martial arts, my body became more and more sensitive. The experience of my body's energy has become very profound. I feel tingles. I feel heat.

Yet there can be others sensations of how someone feels their energy. Someone might feel it as a sense of flowing in their body. For someone else they might experience it as a lightness. For me it feels like a kind of tingling sensation.

Again, the question would be how do you experience your energy? Do you notice energy in your body? The energy itself has its own experience. Notice what it is like when you notice your energy?

MARCEY: By asking this question it takes me out of my head and puts me into my body. In the past I have done exercises where you put your hands in front of you and move them closer together slowly until you can feel the warmth or energy each hand is giving off. Sometimes it almost feels magnetic. It takes me out of my logical part of my brain and then it connects me to the fact that I have this body with this heat in it, with this energy in it; that it is always there. It takes me from my left brain/logical side to my sense and feeling side.

## How Nutrition and Movement Affect Your Physiology

I am not a nutritionist, but I have learned nutrition from my own body. Each person needs to learn nutritionally what are the foods and eating habits that support them best. Beyond optimal health in the body, as you eat better and improve your nutrition, your cognition or mental acuity also improves. There is a link between the foods you eat and how clearly you think. This is why your gut biome is called your second brain. If you would like to explore this topic deeper, see "Gut microbial communities modulating brain development and function" by the National Library of Medicine.

If I eat bread for example, I might get sleepier. If I eat certain cheeses, I know that is not going to go well for me. The work is when you begin to notice for yourself what foods have an effect. How are they affecting how your body feels? How do they affect your body energy? Ultimately, how do they affect your thought processes?

While these types of explorations can be challenging to undertake, it is very effective when someone begins to do this for themselves.

I do not think there is only one way to good health or one kind of diet. You have to optimize your diet for your particular body and optimize what is proper nutrition for yourself. One of the important things from the study of Ayurveda is to understand the assimilation of nutrition. Some people could be eating what seems very healthy, but they might not be getting nourished because their digestion is not breaking down the food properly. They might not be absorbing the nutrients from the healthy food. When that happens, the body treats that undigested food as toxic. Then healthy eating can actually be counter to your health. It is not only starting at the mouth with what you eat, but more importantly how it is getting broken down. Is the food getting fully digested? That is very important to look at, the digestive process and the assimilation process within the small intestine. Are you fully assimilating the nutrients from the food? Did the food get broken down enough so that you have access to the nutrient?

For this you should pay attention to what you feed yourself and how it makes you feel. This ties into your sensitivity, to noticing more and more subtle levels of your experience. You could eat and not notice the effects. But what happens if you start to pay more attention? Can you notice more and more subtly? When you ate that cookie, did it give you a headache? You might not notice the headache right away; it might be very slight. You just munch away on the cookies, but what happens when you stop and notice the effect of the cookie in your body? Can you pay attention and develop your noticing with more levels of subtlety? What about even the process of eating the cookie? What about if we paid attention to how we chewed it, savored it (or not), and the thoughts that go through our head when eating?

> MARCEY: In our culture we are always looking for the external answers. I have seen diet books that encourage eating low fat, low sugar, low carb or a diet based on your blood type. These are a lot of methodologies for

transforming your body. I could imagine that doing any sort of large nutritional shift will have some impact on your body. Your body responds most of the time with some type of weight loss or boosted energy; however, long term it usually does not work. For me it created the pattern of: "I thought this was the external answer that I needed and look, I failed again and my body is bad because it is not responding." At that point it was no longer about the food. Nutrition is complicated because if we subscribe to believing the answer is outside of ourselves with "the experts", we can dismiss our own inner navigation system.

We discussed the body, the uniqueness of each body, and how nutrition can be impactful. It is also very important to put focus on the behaviors of exercise and movement.

When you move the body there are a lot of healthy things that happen. For example, when you move the joints (in any kind of movement), they release synovial fluid which helps lubricate them and keep you flexible. Other forms of movement such as running and certain forms of martial arts can get more extreme and could be challenging for the body—but any kind of movement is helpful for the body. Even simply going on a walk is beneficial.

Movement also helps release serotonin and neurotransmitters that can positively affect your mood and your overall outlook. In terms of types of movement, again it is helpful to find the form that works best for you.

There is a distinction between behavior and movement. Movement is a behavior, but not all behavior is a movement. For example, a behavior could be working on the computer, but that does not require a lot of physical movement. When we talk about movement, we are talking about exercise or a body-based practice, such as yoga, tai chi or dance.

Now let's explore deeper physiology by exploring how your brain actually functions.

## The Neurology of Creating Your Reality and Identity

How does your brain actually create your reality?

The first step is understanding that you create your own reality. When we talk about "reality", it is a nebulous vague word. In our context we will define it as what and how someone is experiencing all the dimensions of their life, their complete orientation and perspectives. Remember that every experience is happening on the inside.

When your mind is creating your experiences, there are specific ways that it does that. If a button is getting pushed or you are having a familiar trigger, how does the mind know how to create and recreate each particular experience? It is through "programs."

Imagine your brain is like a super computer and your experiences are the programs running on that computer. If you want to create change in your experiences, you need to decode the programs and change the way they run. You need to see how you are creating your current reality. The answer: it is neural pathways.

In a neural pathway essentially one neuron touches another neuron which creates a connection for information to travel in your nervous system. While there are a finite number of neurons in your brain and nervous system, there are an infinite number of ways they can interconnect. It has to do with the connections and the phenomenon of getting one neuron to touch a new neuron which creates a new reality.

This reality-creating level is going on very fast in your mind (think fractions of a second). Programs will load up a certain experience within milliseconds. For instance, when all of a sudden you have a reaction that seems to come from out of left field, often it catches you by surprise. Generally, the program, once it loads, will have to complete itself and run its course. If we got into the code of how your brain is creating that program or experience, we find that it is sensory-based information.

Your physical senses are: the eyes, ears, touch, nose, mouth. The content they process are pictures, sounds, feelings (sensations and emotions), smells and tastes.

But your senses also operate internally. Just like you see things externally, you also see things internally, hear things internally and feel things internally. For the sake of brevity, most of the time the olfactory (smell) and gustatory (taste) are not necessarily coming into play as much, but here is an example when olfactory (smell) may trigger a program:

You walk by a bakery and smell a fresh-baked apple pie. You remember the memory of your mom making apple pie when you were a kid. You get a warm fuzzy feeling all over.

In this example, the brain has equated the smell of fresh apple pie with the feeling of being taken care of and nurtured by your mother. This is how the olfactory smell would be the marker for a deeper felt experience.

Most of what you will be dealing with when it comes to transformation and shifting self-limiting patterns is going to be visual, auditory and kinesthetic (body and emotional feelings). It is going to be pictures or images in your mind's eye, sounds or talk in your mind's ear, and emotions or sensations in your body.

From here on out we will use the notation of:

- ▸ **V** for Visual
- ▸ **A** for Auditory
- ▸ **K** for Kinesthetic (meaning felt)
- ▸ **O** for Olfactory
- ▸ **G** for Gustatory

Put them together and we have VAKOG, the label we will use to represent this sensory-level reality. It represents the code for changing your programs.

Everything you could experience in your world is put together by this sensory-based information.

> ⚷ **KEY CONCEPT**
>
> *VAKOG refers to the five senses that we use to collect information that then run through the programs in our brain to create our reality.*

This is what we mean when we say VAKOG. What if you do not have senses? Let us say we wiped your senses clean so you were not seeing anything, hearing anything, or feeling, tasting, or smelling anything. What would be your experience? What happens? There is nothing.

If you want to live by experiencing life in the world, you do that through your senses. Buddhist philosophy tells us there is also a sense attachment. When you get beyond the sense attachment, that is how you begin to get beyond the mind. To know the deeper being that you are you have to see there is an experience that is beyond your senses. We will guide you to that in the third section.

In terms of how you create your reality on a practical level, it is the pictures, sounds, feelings, smells and tastes that are running internally in fractions of a second in your neural pathways. They run in a sequence, are repeatable and are changeable.

When you feel something, how does your brain know to load that particular feeling? It has to have some marker.

As you explore deeper, you find it is usually a memory from the past that acts as the marker; the memory is coded, as an example, in a visual format or maybe I am hearing something (an auditory memory). The memory cues the feeling for the brain. It is fairly consistent.

In my practice when I work on transforming an experience with someone, I watch how they are processing. I am trying to find specific sensory-based information, the memory that is informing the experience. When we discover that memory, there are a number of ways to change how the brain codes it.

For example, you can change what are called the "sub-modalities" of a particular memory. A sub-modality means that when you have a memory, the qualities of that memory, or how it is remembered can be changed. You cannot change the facts of a memory, but you can change the quality of it, how it is remembered. You can also change the emotional charge it may carry.

## Exercise

Think of the last time you were on vacation. Got it? What feelings come up when you remember that vacation? Feel that feeling. Note that just thinking about the vacation creates feelings.

Now in that memory, imagine you had knobs, like controls on an old television. Turn the knobs so that the memory is very, very dim. What happens to the feeling?

**Now this time, turn the knobs up so the memory is very, very bright. What happens?**

**Notice that we are affecting your reality by how your brain is processing the memory.**

**Adjust the knobs until the memory is back to where it originally was.**

**Let us try one more example. Notice how far the memory is from your body. This may sound weird because the memory is happening on the inside. But most of us tend to perceive it as projected somewhere in the sphere around us on the outside.**

**Now move it in closer and farther away, then when you are done, go ahead and bring it back to where it originally was. What changed when you moved the positions?**

**This is how you are creating an experience. The memory (e.g., picture, sound, or feeling) creates a particular feeling and that can be adjusted. This is how "sub-modalities" can be adjusted to change feelings.**

The key is to understand that both your neurology and your physiology are physical in your body. Even though you are processing something mentally, it is happening through a neural pathway and that pathway is physical. The information running in these pathways is the key to transformation. The way to get lasting change is by working at this level of processing by your brain. You have neurological pathways that are running an incredible amount of information. The base code for that information is sensory-based. Everything is coded in your brain in sensory-based data. Let's recap the important points:

- VAKOG is the sense-based information that is running in your brain that you are not seeing.

- VAKOG is what is running on the inside. Your senses see externally but you also see internally, you hear internally, you feel internally.

- VAKOG is bits of information running about 24/bits per second, like a computer language.

If your neurology is the wires, VAKOG is the data. You need to elicit the data to find out what's running. When you do that, you have the keys to changing a program. In order to work on shifting an experience, it is necessary to elicit how the program put together in terms of the sensory based information?

The kinesthetic also dovetails into emotional feelings. There are body feelings and there are also emotional feelings. Your Vs, As, Ks also dictate your behavior. When you notice behavior, you can also notice the accompanying feelings and thoughts. If you drill down and get into the unconscious, you get to the nuts and bolts of how a particular program is running in your neurology. It is the magic of transformation!

When you have a memory, the memory is coded in a visual, auditory or kinesthetic format. Is it a feeling, something you are listening to or something you are seeing? When you are having a particular experience, what are the Vs, As, and Ks that are actually occurring that give rise to that experience? Those Vs, As, and Ks are the code for your memory. Everything in your past is there and was recorded since your birth.

For instance, let's say a person is having a certain reaction. One would look for the "access" point that gives rise to the reaction. This is how to practice transformation by accessing the deeper sensory information that informs each experience.

## ⚷ KEY CONCEPT

*An "access" or "access point" is a means of getting to the key driver for an experience—what actually marks and creates an experience in your brain.*

That's when the deeper structure, whatever it might be, begins to be revealed. It is often something going back to the past. Maybe it was an incident with a parent or the general environment of childhood. When you get into the programs and start to elicit the VAKOG level of information, you will see some of those memories and how they are getting coded. VAKOG is what we call it, but you need to see what the actual content is. You get to the specifics through accessing. An access or access point is a means of getting to the key driver for an experience—what actually marks and creates an experience in your brain. It is getting to the content that informs and directs the brain to "load up" a certain program. Generally, it is from the past and much of the time it is a pain point that has not been resolved. Mostly they are memories.

> MARCEY: Are there general questions that you would ask to help someone access a memory?

> MICHAEL: This is where a practitioner can help elicit that. Maybe in meditation you could access a memory and then work with that. But most of the time, especially if it is a tenacious obstacle, you are not going to see the content. It remains hidden in the unconscious.

There is a limit on how much you can do the unconscious levels of this work by yourself. You absolutely have to take charge of the process and be your own authority, but no human being can see their own blind spots. That is where we need other people. You can only see what you can see, but you cannot see what you are not yet aware of, until you become aware of it. Sometimes that is through self-inquiry and reflection, and sometimes that is through the assistance of others.

We've now set the stage for deeper transformation. It's time to take a look at the way we humans create our own obstacles and how to get beyond them.

# CHAPTER 12

▲ ▲ ▲

# Obstacles Are Opportunities for Transformation

## Your Obstacles Are Inner Experiences

The best way for overcoming your obstacles is by rerouting your neurology. At the end of the day, it is going to be a new neural pathway that is creating a new internal experience for you. For overcoming your obstacles, the focus also needs to be on physiology, the physicality of your experience. It also ties into your behavior, but taking action is secondary to experiencing the internal changes within you.

A lot of people are in their heads. I hear people asking, "Why is this happening to me?" This question can pop you right back into your mental structure, and that is not where you are going to genuinely get any change. Why?

The mind is where the problem is being created. However, it is getting created at the physical level of the mind which is usually an aspect of the unconscious mind. Remember, mind is not separate from body. The interface for body and mind is at the neurological level with your brain and nervous system, the physical components of your mind. How then do you gain access to this level of your experiences?

The secret lies in being able to determine how your brain is doing what it is doing (remember VAKOG).

Most obstacles are internal. This is the point—it is not so much the outer obstacle itself, but how your obstacles are getting created at the level of your neurology. What is your actual experience when you encounter an obstacle? While outer obstacles do exist, every outer obstacle is going to have an inner experience to it.

For example, the outer obstacle could be "I need resources", or "I need more financing for my endeavor." Of course there is some attention that has to be placed outside yourself in terms of the obstacle; you cannot ignore that. However, when you encounter an obstacle, you are also having an inner experience to that particular obstacle. You can make obstacles more difficult or easy. There is the obstacle itself, but how you approach it makes a big difference.

**🔑 KEY CONCEPT**

*While outer obstacles exist, they have an inner experience that is self-created. Deconstructing this can bring a powerful shift in your consciousness and give you the opportunity to have a more positive experience.*

In some cases, there are obstacles about which you may have no choice, for example, if someone is born without a limb, or has a mental disability, or loses a loved one. For obstacles such as these, there may be nothing one can do to change the circumstances, but one can work with them on adjusting how one may accept, adapt, grow and even thrive with the obstacle. If you are in a situation that you cannot change, you can work with how you live with it.

In another category however, there are the self-created obstacles, the ones in which you do have a choice and can make a change. Deconstructing these obstacles can bring a powerful shift in your consciousness and give you the opportunity to have a more positive experience.

Some obstacles that you might think are outside of your control are in fact changeable. In order to change those that can be changed, you need to get into the unconscious. You need to peer beneath the surface. You need to see the pattern or structure of your inner experiences of your obstacles. You need to see how you are actually creating the experience.

For many people it is their internal feelings that are the obstacles. Maybe someone's outer circumstances are fine, but they feel pain or issues on the inside. Some obstacles have to do with identity, the mental notions of self. These types of obstacles can be self-limiting or self-inflating. In the self-limiting type someone is erroneously believing something that devalues or limits who they think they are. In the self-inflating type, someone is trying to bolster or expand who they think they are. Both are ultimately rooted in a lie about self.

No one is greater or lesser than anyone else. When you debunk the lies that you have come to believe about yourself, you can live more authentically as your true self.

> MARCEY: Are you talking about everyday things that cause problems such as finances, relationships, work, housing, dealing with difficult people?

> MICHAEL: We could name 100 different examples of obstacles. Everyone references their obstacles in a different way. Maybe having difficulties with focus could be an obstacle. Or not having enough money could be an obstacle. Maybe one's communication is the obstacle. Again, there could be 100 different examples of obstacles. However, the focus does not need to be on examples as much as on how the obstacles are getting created in your neurology and making a distinction between obstacles that you can change and obstacles that you cannot change.

First, what are the obstacles to which you can apply a transformative process and experience change so that the obstacles cease to exist?

Second, can you shift your focus to how the obstacle is getting created? Have your focus be not so much on the obstacle itself but on the process of shifting the obstacle.

Let's focus on the process of making change. If there is an obstacle that you are struggling with, asking yourself these types of questions can be useful:

▷ Is it something that I can change?

▷ What is within my control? And what is out of my control?

▷ What if this were an opportunity rather than an obstacle?

▷ Where does this experience originate from?

▷ How is it getting created?

▷ What would it be like if I were already beyond this obstacle?

What we discuss in the rest of this chapter relates to the obstacles where you can make a change. This is really the transformative aspect of the book...the nuts and bolts of what you can do to get positive changes.

When we talk about obstacles, the focus does not have to be on obstacles themselves, but on how to get through them, to shift them, and the techniques to do it.

Noticing and recognizing the patterns of obstacles and seeing the ones rooted in your identity has the biggest impact. When you do that, if you want change, it has to get down to that sensory-based information. You also must access any memory or memories relevant to the situation at hand.

## ⚷ KEY CONCEPT

*You can have an impact on obstacles that show up in your life if you begin to notice and recognize patterns of obstacles and any memories relevant to them.*

The self-created obstacles continue as obstacles because there is more content below the threshold of your awareness—content that you are not accessing. We have already discussed the unconscious mind. If you sincerely want to change something, if you genuinely want the obstacle to be transcended, you have to go into the unconscious mind and find the reference points for how it is getting created.

The inquiry is: How are you actually doing that?

What if you took the judgment out of it (using acceptance) and simply asked how something is occurring for you? Once you do this, you start to discover the keys to shift your experiences and your reality.

This is one instance where it may help to have a guide. Everyone has blind spots in their awareness. An adept outside guide can watch you. They can watch how you are processing, and can pick up physiological cues, and guide you to see how you are processing those visual, auditory and kinesthetic pieces of information at the unconscious level. To start this yourself you can ask:

▸ What is the picture running through my mind when I have a particular experience?

▸ What do I hear in my "mind's ear"?

▸ What are the feelings or emotions that I have with this particular experience?

▸ What sensations occur in my body?

A good guide shows you how to unpack the deeper parts of an experience, and then how to metaphorically "move the wires around." That is where some of the magic and art along with practice of this work comes in... how to do that. The tools given in this book are a good start and might need learning and practicing over time.

We are giving you the tools, and it takes practice to use them effectively; so be patient!

Overcoming an obstacle involves creating a new experience at the internal sensory level (VAKOG). You are running a neural pathway that gives rise to your experience of an obstacle. When you change the neural pathway, you change the obstacle. That is the whole essence of what we are talking about here. There is not an obstacle other than how you are creating it. Overcoming it means deconstructing how your brain is doing what it is doing and reconstructing a new, more useful program.

Once you notice a pattern that is changeable and you want to change a particular obstacle, you first need to notice, listen and accept more.

As you do that, you begin to notice more of the unconscious content, more of how your brain creating it. Think of the experience as a program running in your brain. The brain is working properly. It is not a hardware issue. It is the software. It is a program running in your brain that is doing what it is supposed to do. Even if the outcome is negative or self-limiting, the program is still working properly. Somehow along the way it got designed that way. Seeing how it was created brings to light what was hidden and will make the unconscious conscious. Try to see what is happening in this obstacle creation. See what is happening below the threshold of your everyday awareness.

As you practice, start to notice that your unconscious mind and your body reflect each other. They have a link to each other. Your memories inform your present. Your brain is generally running information through your memory filters which give rise to the obstacles. In order to change you have to go back and access the core imprints, the core wounding, the core learnings, the events that happened in the past that are giving rise to the obstacles in the present.

Again, we call these access points. These are the particular inner images or the particular memories that inform your reality. Whatever is informing your obstacle experience, that is what you access. Thus, you can practice transformation through accessing these points.

> MARCEY: There is something that you touched on which was how the unconscious mind and the body reflect each other.

> MICHAEL: The body is a fast track to making the unconscious conscious. It is like seeing a reflection. How do you see the unconscious? If something is unconscious, you are obviously not aware of that by the very nature of the name. So how then do you make the unconscious conscious? There are different ways to do that. You can look for the access, but you can also go through your body and see how it is responding to a particular reference point. How does it feel? What does your energy do? Typically, that is going to get you very quick to the unconscious content. Because the body will reflect the unconscious parts of your experiences.

When I was younger, I suffered from a lot of depression. If I wanted to get very quickly into the depressed state, the body does it the quickest. Through my body I could notice how my shoulders hunch forward, and my head drops down and my core collapses. I could go instantly into that experience through the body. It is a way to see what is happening very quickly.

It is the same with behavior. Behavior is the best indicator of someone's true intention. One could say, "I want to treat people kindly" and then they snap at people all day long. Well, the true intention is they want to snap at people because that is what they are living out.

This is an opportunity for deeper awareness. Remember, the mind loves to tell a story. You can tell yourself a story about anything. That does not mean it is going to get a pattern to change. How do you see what is really occurring? One way is to go through the body. You also have to go to your memory banks and look at how memories are creating a certain reality for you or a certain obstacle for you.

> MARCEY: That is interesting. Could it work conversely, by bringing confidence with shoulders back, standing tall and deep breathing?

> MICHAEL: Yes, however, the old pattern is still going to exist. You cannot put a new pattern over an old pattern. You have to remove or revise the old pattern and then install the new pattern. When you have two patterns that are in conflict, the deeper one wins.

That is why the law of attraction does not work for certain people because they are only using their conscious mind. They are saying, "I want to create this wonderful life for myself", and then unconsciously they are believing and doing things counter to that.

If you want to create change, you have to see what is happening under the threshold of your awareness. What is happening below the surface?

## 🔑 KEY CONCEPT

*The Law of Attraction does not work if there are unconscious beliefs counter to what you wish to attract.*

How are you creating a particular experience running through your memory banks in your neurology by way of the visual, auditory and kinesthetic information that give rise to a particular experience? I'll repeat that over and over again until you see that it is information running in your neurology at fractions of a second. If the information is from your past and you have not revised it yet, that program will keep running automatically.

Additionally, there are layers to those past experiences. You have progressed in your awareness as an adult, but the deeper layers continue to operate. Imagine there are versions of you at different ages: you at one, you at five years old, you at seven, at ten, fifteen, up to your current age. Each of these "yous" are stacked in a hierarchical fashion and are informing your present-day you. You are being informed by the past versions yourself and your experiences.

Everything you are thinking, feeling and doing is running through your memory filters. If you want to change it, you have to go through and change how those memories get processed. You have to change how the information runs in your brain.

That does not mean changing the facts of your past. The facts aren't going to change but the experience of those facts can indeed change. Say someone believes they are no good because their parents neglected them. That is an obstacle. They are going to be living life trying to compensate for that. This particular person might try to prove their worth, but underneath it is the original lack of value and the belief that "I am not worth it because my parents did not give me attention."

If they want to change that, nothing is going to change the fact that their parents did not give them attention. But they can change how they referenced themselves when that fact occurred. They could experience themselves as valid and that it was the parents' problem. Because they weren't seen and validated has nothing to do with who they authentically are. Everyone has value as a human being. Once you get that new information into the access point, that is it. The change is done.

What we are laying out here is that the obstacle is a neural pathway and a filter of how you are perceiving your reality. When you are experiencing the obstacle, see how the obstacle is getting created from your past and how it is happening in your brain. This is the magic of the inside and a powerful way this book provides you.

## Working with Obstacle Patterns

When we talk about patterns, we are referring to repeating patterns, the stuff we want to change. In the context of what can be transformed, the repeating pattens are the ones that have the biggest impact.

> MARCEY: When neuropathways are used often or over a long period of time, they become stronger. Is it safe to assume that for someone who is trying to overcome a

pattern that, as they get older, the pathways get much deeper than for a younger person?

MICHAEL: Yes. It has to do with how much the pathway is used. It is not a consequence of your age but the consequence of being alive longer. You would have used that particular pathway more throughout your life.

For transformation to happen you have to recognize the pattern and you have to see the underlying structure of the experience. At this point it involves a deeper noticing.

 **KEY CONCEPT**

*Transforming your experiences requires seeing the underlying structure within the experience.*

For pattern recognition you can see that something is repeating itself and that the experience has a structure to it.

One may notice, "Every time this particular event happens, I have the same feeling come up." That is one aspect of what we mean by pattern recognition. Yet recognition also means noticing patten structure.

## Pattern Structure

What is pattern structure? This is a very transformative question to ask. It gets down to how an experience is put together at the sensory level of our neurology (VAKOG).

When we talk about structure, it is the physical, emotional and mental pieces put together and how they operate as a whole.

Consider an indoor wall for example. What you see is a flat wall that is usually painted. If you break through the sheetrock, you find beams nailed together and other wooden braces—it is the physical structure within the wall that determines its outer shape.

The form is what you see on the outside (the painted wall), but the structure is what gives rise to the form from the inside (the beams). When you want to reprogram an obstacle or reprogram a pattern, you need to elicit that structure to be able to shift the outer parts.

MARCEY: For someone who is not familiar with working with this VAKOG level, let us say I realize that I am
reacting to something as my normal response. To notice:
would I then stop and do an assessment by noticing that
it came up and then by thinking about what triggered
me? Would I ask myself how my body is feeling? What
questions would I be asking myself? For example, sometimes when my family comes home at the same time and
I have been home alone, all of a sudden I feel stressed.
Everybody's bringing their own energy home and I get
triggered. I notice on my low days my response can be
anything from isolating in my room to eating something
that makes me feel better.

MICHAEL: That stress reaction has a structure to it—
how is that getting created in your brain? There is a
stimulus (something outside yourself), but it pushes a
button inside yourself. In this example, there is an internal program called your stress response.

Now part of that could be natural to your being. You could
be authentically sensitive, in a way that does not need to change
because it is part of who you are to respond in that way. But it could
also be a behavioral pattern that could be changed. One might want
to have better choices on how to deal with the event of everyone
coming home at once. If you do not want to go into eating or isolating, you need to have some better choices.

You could challenge it and say, "Okay, maybe the stress response
isn't authentic. I want to revise that." Then you would need to
explore how the stress is getting created. How are you doing that?
Guess what the answer is. VAKOG!

Typically, when you stress...

There is a *sensation* in your body to the stress.

There is an *emotional aspect* to what goes along with the stress
(maybe some memories).

There is a set of *thinking aspects* that go along with the stress
(the actual Vs and As that inform the memories).

If you go down deep enough, there are *certain beliefs* about what you think or assume is occurring in that stress.

There is usually a lot more going on under the surface. You could say, "I am stressed", or you could begin to challenge it and begin to unpack the whole program called stress.

Something external happens. It is more than a general stressful situation; it is "Marcey's Stress Button" that was created and manifests in a specific way. It is very specific to the individual and then from that one could start checking internally, continuing to go deeper. That stress button was pushed and intellectually, maybe you can reflect on what happened, but then the next level is: "What is the sensation in my body? How do I feel emotionally? What beliefs are surrounding this and where does that come from?"

Can you start to become curious and notice the pattern and how it breaks down for you? What appears to be external (family comes home) eventually gets down into your own internal belief system.

It is the full internal experience that you want to elicit or unpack. When you have the necessary information by getting down to those specific Vs, As, and Ks, then you have the keys to change it around.

### Example of Working Through the Inquiry Questions with a Client

| | |
|---|---|
| Situation: | A friend came over to help with a project, but when they showed up, they were having a bad day and were in a bad mood. The client needed their friend's help, but ended up getting so impatient they had a hard time getting the project done because the person helping was so distracting. |
| Feelings? Emotions? | I started feeling anxious. |
| Sensation? | My heart started beating a little faster. |
| Threat Aspect? | On high alert, I was no longer relaxed. |

| Thinking Aspects, Beliefs? | After reflection, I realized that I am a type of person who empathizes and feels like I match other people's energy level. If you come and meet me, and you are easygoing, laidback, and chill, I match that and will be in a laidback chill state. If you show up at my house and start doing stuff with me, but you were having a bad day, my natural inclination is to meet that energy level and be upset with you. |
|---|---|
| | In talking about it, I am realizing it would be a much better situation if I was able to maintain my joy or optimal state, even around people that are bringing a different type of energy. |

When you are looking for the VAKOG access, take it with a grain of salt because the content can sometimes be tricky to catch. Again, it is a neural pathway running very fast. You can have a moment of clarity where suddenly you realize what a whole pattern is about. The content presents itself. Yet it is sometimes very hard to catch the Vs, As, and Ks, mostly the Vs and As. You can usually catch the feelings, but you are not usually aware of the actual thought forms, the pictures and sounds (also internal self-talk) running very fast and below the level of your everyday awareness.

If you think of it as a thought form, it is the form of your thinking that can be hard to catch. Mostly, you are aware that you are thinking and usually also aware of the content, what you are thinking about. But what happens when you ask the questions, "How are you thinking? What is the form of the thinking?"

Do you think in pictures? Do you think more in terms of what you are hearing in your head? Or is it processing the emotion without a lot of thought? This is different for everyone and everyone has their comfort place. This is part of the exploration. Regardless of your preferred thinking style, one of the things that is consistent for each program is the body, the feeling and the mental piece. It is how the three go together that creates a total experience.

MARCEY: On the example above, this new understanding was probably helpful for your client to notice. Then they could start noticing their mood and energy level around others.

MICHAEL: Yes! Then they can start to ask themselves what is going on deeper.

These questions can be used as a template. It may not answer every question, but it can serve as a guide, so that as you explore deeper aspects, and you begin to have the awareness around your own experience. This is something that each of us can learn to do. You can gain much by working with the process and with your own inquiry.

If you want to debunk a neural program, ask yourself what you are feeling. What is the sensation? What are you looking at in your mind's eye or hearing in your mind's ear? Do you recall any memories associated with this experience? What are the components of each of these, so you can start to break down a specific pattern?

In the example above, my client knew the feeling as anxiety, then the sensation was a racing heart. Those are helpful pieces of information, and when you bring them together in the same space, you create awareness and awakening. In this approach you notice as much as possible in order to see how you are creating your own reality and how to change it.

The question to ask is, "What is really happening?" In the client example, they become more aware of the experience and start to notice more. They then can get deeper by getting to the sensory based information (VAKOG). But they also notice what is happening on the safety/threat level of their brain. Something of this nature gets coded as a threat, a threat to their peace and stability. Even though it is not an actual threat, when that stressed-out person shows up, their brain reacts to it the same way. The sensation is an indication of danger, that something does not feel safe here.

A lot of times you can bring it back to safety. When you are working with transforming an obstacle, much of the problem could be that you are not feeling safe at the fight-or-flight level. This part of your brain is the "gatekeeper." Once you get through that, then you get to the experience itself. Many people code the painful parts of their experiences as unsafe to allow into their consciousness. In that case they create resistance to moving beyond the obstacle. The brain is working properly to keep the content out of awareness. This is why safety is important. We mention this in reference to not only developing rapport with the people around you, but also within yourself as well.

What is it like when you feel safe enough within yourself to see things that might not feel safe?

After exploring deeply this example, it is time to go deeper down into the unconscious and the real reason change does not occur—unconscious attachments.

## Working with the Unconscious Attachments of Obstacle Patterns

*"One does not become enlightened by imagining figures of light, but by making the darkness conscious."*
~Carl Jung

It is not what you are aware of that keeps an obstacle in place; it is what you are not aware of. You have to get into the unconscious mind, get into what is not being seen, in order to effectively get through an obstacle (especially if it is a tough one). Sometimes if it is a small thing, you can muscle through it or make a new choice. But if it is an extremely tenacious obstacle, there is almost always an unconscious attachment to it.

### ⚷ KEY CONCEPT

*It is not what you are aware of that is the problem; it is what you are not aware of. Tenacious obstacles almost always have an unconscious attachment that you are not aware of.*

Earlier we talked about people asking, "Why is this happening?" and then they go back into their mental structure, but the response is getting created at multiple levels. When you encounter experiences that are more difficult, how do you start uncovering that unconscious attachment?

Unconscious attachments could be referenced to under the banner of:

**"ALL THE REASONS WHY YOU ACTUALLY WANT AN EXPERIENCE THAT YOU CONSCIOUSLY DO NOT WANT AND HOW IT HAS BENEFITED YOU IN WAYS THAT YOU MAY NOT BE AWARE OF!"**

The attachment at the unconscious level is saying there is some value to a certain experience, be it positive or negative. Yes, you can unconsciously value negative experiences.

When you have a painful experience, then the attachment is that there is some value to having that experience. It says that you have to keep creating the experience in your world because of how it works on some level—the attachments that you are not yet aware of. There might be alliances, loyalties and potential payoffs that keep you bound unconsciously.

Take a particular painful experience such as being scapegoated by family members. The attachment could involve family loyalties to their ancestors. Maybe one of the ancestors was scapegoated and that dynamic continues to propagate within the family because the members remain unaware of how it started. This type of attachment is from family systems work which we explain in more detail in the next chapter. You can get caught in loyalties such as these outside of your conscious awareness.

If you have worked on a painful issue and are not able to shift it, it is possible that unconscious attachments were developed from loyalty to your own family system. There might be an unwritten rule in your family that said everyone has to have some portion of whatever that particular issue is. Family attachments are some of the most powerful, but unconscious attachments can happen for multiple reasons. Again, the driver is that you unconsciously want the painful experience regardless of the reason.

Attachments are like little bungee cords to your experiences. They pull it back when you try to move out of the experience. You try to let it go, but those bungee cords pull it right back in. Attachments are the reasons why you want to keep your pain and obstacles.

If something is not completely resolved, it is going to come up repetitively. A common complaint from clients is why things keep coming up over and over and over again. The answer is that usually there is an unconscious attachment that they may not know about until we begin to look at them.

One way you can get to them quickly is look at what is showing up in your world.

As an example, let's say someone keeps having to deal with abusive people in their life. For whatever reason they keep attracting bullies. They may say, "No, no! That is the last thing I want. I want people who love and respect me." However, what they have is internal programming that is either a victim or a rescuer (remember the triangle from Part One), so their brain keeps recreating the experience and the attachment to the experience. The attachment is something that the person may not be in touch with - they only know that bullies keep showing up.

An additional inquiry question is: How does it benefit you to have this happening?

An answer of "there's no benefit" avoids looking deeper. It may not benefit you on the conscious level but there is benefit on the unconscious level. Flipping it around and looking at the benefit is a way to work with the attachments; however, most people do not like to do it. They recognize that they do not want a certain experience, but the experience continues to get created. Thus, there is a part of their unconscious that does want it on some level more deeply than they know.

Sometimes when you start this shift, it is possible to feel a sense of loss. In a strange way, something very painful can be valued in the heart. How would you recognize that? Typically, people are not consciously aware of that.

Let's take a look a real-life example from one of my client sessions:

> Client: I tried the exercise of sitting quietly and listening to my body and something that seemed like an unconscious program came up. It was the realization that in my family there are many people that like to side with the underdog, the less powerful, or they take the side (for right or wrong) of the contrarian. They are big fans of

rooting for the underdog. As an adult, I can now understand that I sometimes play small and have to stay the underdog in a weird way to get support. When I do find success, that means there is an underdog on the other side who's not doing as well, who usually usurps the support of my family from me.

Michael: What would it be like if, let's say, there was a shift in the system? What would it be like for you if you could have success and support? You could be the winner and feel support at the same time.

Client: I cannot even grasp that in a weird way. I would love that. I think I have that from friends.

Michael: It is okay and may be helpful to realize that the support is there, but not from the family of origin. What is your identity when you are neither the underdog nor the champion—not over or under?

Client: That feels like an experience of something bigger that the success itself—a connection to something greater. Or another reason for doing what I am doing. It feels like energy, not body, not mind, like being a part of a greater system.

Michael: I think that is a way on to your mountaintop. Detachment from needing to be under or over. You do not need to prove this success in life. You are trying to counter being an underdog and you do not need to be an underdog for the support. You can dis-identify with both of those identities and be in that greater mountaintop experience of being neither under nor over.

Then you take that and go back to the system. Imagine going back to your mom when you were a child, and tell her that it is okay, that you do not need to play this game to get support. You found it somewhere else. Then you can open up the new filter in your mind where the other conscious people in your life love you as you are, and support you as you are without needing to be under or over; no proving is necessary—in any of it.

Client: My family is fantastic at rallying when someone is down, but are not big on celebrating achievements, and I am constantly chasing that success.

Michael: Is being down a way to rally the family?

Client: Yes, for sure.

Michael: Then you have to look: Is there a hidden dimension of you as a child that takes on the mission to be the one who rallies? What is it like when you let go of that and realize that was never your job? It is a loss, right? It is the loss of a beautiful mission, a beautiful intent, and you are also letting everything be in the original imperfect state of affairs. However, once you let go of the mission, then there's no more scorecard. There's no more rallying—it simply drops off the map.

Your mind does not like that because those old experiences are known reference points. It leads you into the mystical state, because now you are in something much greater that does not have these known markers. Yet you can go back from that mystical state and create new markers in your body-mind, but it is not necessary. You could also live more in the mystical state without needing those old markers.

The key is looking at the unconscious attachments to what was the potential payoff as a child when you were the underdog, and you rallied the troops by being the underdog. What would it have been like if you could have been recognized for your efforts of being the one to bring the family together? It is the loss of that grand mission that you can begin to reference—understanding that you can no longer be that. It is not reflecting who you are today. It is an identity. It is an identity—the Savior identity.

Client: I started to notice this concept during a time when I was calm and had a calm mind. It opened up something in my unconscious.

Michael: Begin to reference the attachment, the old attachment, to those known reference points. What is it like when you are letting those go? What is the experience of releasing the known attachments even though they were painful and difficult? What is it like to let those go?

Client: It feels like there are these tie-downs that I can cut. I see a picture in my mind of balloons that get cut and they float into the sky—as if they are freed.

Michael: What does that feel like in your body?

Client: It feels lighter, like less responsibility, less being tied to things that I do not want to be tied to.

Michael: Fantastic.

Hopefully, this illustrated how the unconscious can keep us bound. As I mentioned, it takes time and practice. But once you begin the practice, the recognition of the unconscious happens more easily. Let's now explore some examples that tend to be common for many of us. First, we will explore some commonly known obstacles, ones that tend to be more conscious for many of us, and then some hidden ones that tend to be less understood, ones that tend to remain unconscious, thus can be more tenacious to shift. While the number of obstacles we can experience is broad, we're only going to focus on a few key ones here. This isn't a comprehensive list of the obstacles we might encounter, but are some key ones that could be beneficial to understand and work with.

## Overcoming Common Obstacles

This section might be a bit more challenging for some readers. But by approaching it with acceptance, you can develop the ability to look at obstacles that many of us encounter as well as your own personal ones.

One important point as we enter into this next section is to take it with a grain of salt. It is okay to keep it light and not take everything to heart. These are frames and overlays for experiences I have seen come up with people. That does not mean all of these examples are going to apply to every person We remind you to use it if it helps and throw it out if it does not apply. It is not necessary to sit in these obstacles for too long while reading this section. The next chapter will focus on the transformational tools that you can use to transform some of these obstacles. We start by addressing some of the more common obstacles. Again this list by no means covers all the obstacles people could encounter. It is merely meant to give a starting point by looking at three of the more common obstacles: triggering, habits and addictions.

## Triggering

Triggering is a term we use to describe getting your buttons pushed. There are different kinds of triggers. First, there are the ones that are authentic to each person. For example, if someone comes up and tries to take a swipe at you for some unknown reason, it's normal to be triggered—real time, right then. That would be a very authentic trigger. It is an immediate threat and the brain responds as such.

## ⚷ KEY DEFINITION

*Trigger: A stimulus that elicits a reaction. For example, an event could be a trigger for a memory of a past experience and an accompanying state of emotional arousal.*
*~American Psychological Association*

Then there are the triggers where the internal reaction is not congruent with the outside cause. For example, if you feel intense rage when your partner leaves the cap off the toothpaste, there is probably something there to look at because the outside behavior is not significant enough to cause such a reaction.

You can see there are different types of triggers and that is where discernment should be used. You have to determine for yourself whether or not a trigger needs more attention and possibly needs to be reprogrammed.

One of the first things to understand is that it is alright to get triggered regardless of the reason. Sometimes we make the triggering bad or wrong, but it is going to happen. There is nothing wrong because it's part of our neurology.

When we get triggered, how do we get back to our place of peace and internal calmness as soon as possible?

If you feel threatened whether it be real or imagined, the trigger is a natural fight/flight/freeze response and the best way to regain your composure is to work with your breath. Focus on deepening your breathing pattern and focus your mind on the fact that, once the threat has passed, you are safe. The breath is always the most important factor in regaining your peace whenever you are triggered.

If you have determined that the trigger involves an incongruent reaction, then after calming down, begin to explore what is happening deeper within you regarding your reaction. Sometimes the situation may feel dangerous even if it is not an actual threat. Much of the time it is coming from the past and can be reprogrammed by working with the structure of the experience. You can work with triggers by learning about the reaction when it happens. Start to unpack what is happening within you in the moment. Explore what is happening in your attachment to the trigger and with any unconscious need to have the reaction (for instance, is it just an unresolve temper tantrum form your childhood?).

> MARCEY: It seems like I am either on the mountaintop, feeling great, or confronted by obstacles in my day-to-day life, feeling far from the mountaintop energy. Even though I am feeling better and more peace day-to-day, I am still getting triggered and sometimes pretty badly, where I feel as if I am broadsided. Does getting triggered ever go away completely?

> MICHAEL: Sometimes we are broadsided by a situation outside ourselves when we are not expecting it—where something comes from out of left field and suddenly, we are triggered. This can happen even after we reprogram a trigger because the original neural pathway still exists. The potential of the trigger button is in there, but the reaction might no longer be an issue. The trigger might happen and it gets easier to return to your mountaintop.

Remember that as we explore obstacles in this section, we are doing it in a context of making that mountaintop experience more easily accessible, always in service of our greater journey and our greater good. That is why we are bringing obstacles up—it is not a focus specifically on the obstacle itself, but how to get through them, how they are occurring and why it is okay to have them.

Sometimes triggered reactions continue to happen repeatedly. There can be an unconscious hook inside that keeps it happening over and over. By learning more when triggers are occurring, you can start to notice if there is a core wound associated with the trigger. Instead of spiraling on the surface of your experience, you can begin to more quickly bring your attention to a deeper level of understanding. This means understanding whether or not there is a core wound to work with in that moment when a trigger fires off.

If there is a wound, your consciousness is trying to bring your attention to what that is and how the trigger is occurring. That is why sometimes jerks show up to push our buttons because it is a compassionate act of your own consciousness to get you in touch with what needs healing. With practice you can more easily notice what needs attention. You can foster a sense of inner safety and experience less triggering as you progress.

## Habits

The more you do a specific behavior or run a specific internal state, the more your body begins to use the neural pathway. The more you use a specific neural pathway, the more it becomes habitual. A habit is when there is a repetitive action involved. Habits tend to run on autopilot.

For most habits, with some intention, you can break the habit with willpower. Typically, it takes twenty-one days to develop a new neurological connection. If you are wanting to break a habit, a good way to look at it is not stopping what you are doing, but starting something new that is counter to the old habit - that is going to be more effective. What is important is to replace the old behavior with a new behavior. Again, most habits can be shifted with an intention. With a habit you have a choice.

However, there is a difference between habits and addictions.

## Addictions

Everyone has habits and humans are habitual by nature.

There is a specific set of habits called addictions. The difference between a habit and an addiction is that people do not have a choice over the behavior with an addiction. They are powerless over the behavior. When we run a neural pathway, the more we use that pathway, the more the body begins to bolster it, wrap it, and make it more robust.

If we run a neural pathway the same way constantly, it becomes stronger. Like water running down a hillside, it cuts a groove deeper and deeper each time it is used. Addiction has a much deeper impact.

> **🔑 KEY DEFINITION**
>
> *Habit: A well-learned behavior or automatic sequence of behaviors that is relatively situation specific and over time has become motorically reflexive and independent of motivational or cognitive influence—that is, it is performed with little or no conscious intent*
> *~American Psychological Association*

> **🔑 KEY DEFINITION**
>
> *Addiction: A state of psychological or physical dependence (or both) on the use of alcohol or other drugs. The term is often used as an equivalent term for substance dependence and sometimes applied to behavioral disorders, such as sexual, Internet, and gambling addictions*
> *~American Psychological Association*

Addictions can also be classified as a spiritual malady usually having to do with a sense of powerlessness. When there is addiction, there is an existential crisis that the person is going through, usually an empty feeling on the inside or some pain on the inside that the person is avoiding. When we get to the level of addiction, the problem is that willpower does not work anymore. The person in the throes of addiction loses choice and the addiction becomes disempowering. A lot of times people will be in addiction because they are feeling powerless or empty underneath it. The addictive behavior gives a momentary sense of relief—the behavior becomes a momentary salve.

The addiction, whatever it is—shopping, food, alcohol, drugs—becomes a salve to keep the person from having to face the inner realm. Neurologically, the behavior and the pleasure you get from indulging in your addiction runs through the pleasure center and your body releases serotonin and dopamine.

Two things happen when you begin to get out of addiction. One is you have to face the tolerance that has been created. Tolerance is the bodies' way of adapting to greater and greater levels of the addiction. It builds up over time and when you stop the addictive behavior there is a backlash from the withdrawal as the body chemistry readjusts. Usually, the withdrawal is enough to push people right back into the addictive behavior. If you get past the first couple of days of any addiction, it typically gets easier.

Once you have dealt with the backlash of withdrawal, then you have to examine the underlying condition. What is the underlying pain, issue or condition that initially caused the addictive behavior?

It is a tougher nut to crack when it gets into addiction because you cannot choose your way out or use willpower to get over it. If you could, it would just be a habit. That is the problem with addiction; it is a loss of willpower. One does not have the choice to get out of it.

Most of the models, for example, the twelve-step model, use a spiritual orientation on dealing with this. They say that you are powerless and should rely on a power greater than yourself. That is part of healing—knowing that there is something greater than self to help you get out of addiction. Whether it be group, partnership, community, advocacy, therapy... whatever it is... it is important that you are working with something greater than self. When it comes to addiction, it is wise to seek assistance.

For me personally, the twelve-step program did not work very well. While parts of it helped greatly (especially the higher power piece), when I explored it, it did not resonate. Most of my impetus to heal my addictions was from having a momentary awakening—a moment of clarity. It was a moment of a better experience and what was possible.

What about an addiction that seems to be healed, then there is a relapse? Could addiction be something engrained in one's DNA?

At the core of this spiritual malady is usually a spiritual emptiness. We are not talking about the Buddhist use of emptiness; we are talking about existential emptiness which is very painful. It means people at their center feel as though there is nothing to life, that there is no meaning. Rather than go through that pain and find a deeper truth at a deeper level, they externalize to something outside themselves. In doing so they do not have to face their pain.

What about people who just stop the addictive behavior?

There is no rhyme or reason in terms of the human experience. There is no single formula for getting through these types of obstacles. In certain situations one could call it *grace*. Did the change come from one's own free will or was there the "something more" factor, some grace? Most of the spiritual aspects of healing come from grace or something that comes from God or a higher power. It is something beyond understanding which seems to happen.

In my own journey that is the only way I have been able to get through it, and I still grapple with it. For me I remind myself to "let go and let God" (from the twelve steps). If I trust Spirit and the love within me, it keeps me on my journey.

Isolation and loneliness are big drivers in addiction as well. People do not want to face an inner loneliness so the addiction covers that over. The antidote at that point would be connection and community. Sometimes this is what draws people out of addiction—when you start to have some sort of connection, friends, family or community, something better to replace it.

What about the concept of hitting rock bottom? Is there an option of self-examination, of peeling back layers and observing behavior and the drivers that can help uncover what needs to be healed?

The hardest thing about addiction is having to go it alone. People try to keep their addictions hidden. There is an expectation that we have it all together, but the more we can talk about it and bring it to the light of day, the more we realize that there is no shame in having an addiction. What would it be like if we could begin to expose these aspects and feel safe enough to share this with the people in our lives?

## Working with Addictions

If someone is struggling with addiction, it helps to look at it is an opportunity for awakening. They may not have to hit rock bottom. Instead, some come through addiction by doing the inner work, by digging and finding out what is going on without having to crash. Some people do crash as an impetus to get out of the addiction, but that is a hard path to travel.

Some addicts believe that if they just got over the addiction, then life will be perfect and euphoric. This is an example of self-deception which is one of the biggest factors in maintaining addiction. Self-deception is the lies we tell ourselves. "Everything is fine if I just keep busy." "I am clear even though I have this behavior or habit that I cannot control", or whatever the story is. The narrative helps keep the addictive behavior in place.

We need to challenge our beliefs around it, to challenge the behavior around it. It is a calling to reconnect with our authentic center. At the end of the day the only thing that works is to stop.

It is not only stopping the behavior, but it is stopping everything. It is hitting the pause button on your life for a moment so that you can stop and experience what is going on at a deeper level in yourself. Pause for a moment. In that pause that is where you begin to get awareness. That is where spirit can come in. Something more can come in and do that work of grace to assist you in that journey.

Remember that we can get caught up in the story by asking why something is happening; that question can cause the mind to continue to spin. What if you were to sit and feel what is going on? This may be new and uncomfortable, but try to hold off from analyzing or asking why. Instead sit and feel whatever feelings that come up.

For some the practice of stopping or getting out of our thoughts and connecting to the message in our bodies will start to bring insight and may bring the little pieces of the puzzle back together.

In addition, it is crucial that you have to have something to replace the behavior with, because if not, you can be left with your own mind. I have noticed one of the hardest things (after I go through a couple days and clean out my body) is my mind starts to spin around in justification. I can find my mind

 **KEY CONCEPT**

*It is important to replace unwanted behaviors with something wanted, or else once the unwanted behavior is not there the mind can be left to spin.*

saying, "Okay, I have achieved the clarity, so now I am done, right?" What an illusion that can be.

What about dealing with the deeper feelings of deprivation as they relate to addiction?

Consider the phrase, "I want what I want when I want it." I do not think it is useful when people use the word "deserve"—I deserve this or that. Sometimes it is healthy to deprive ourselves of indulgences. It is not necessarily healthy to indulge in every desire because you want it right now. It is your right but it may not be the best course of action for you.

What happens with addiction is that there is a deep desire—there is a desire for pleasure or for comfort or for relief. People feel that desire and then they act on the desire. But this is a distortion of desire. If you sit long enough with the craving and aching for an addiction, eventually you will see what you want, the "something else" beneath it—comfort, safety, security, connection. Then you can ask yourself, "Where is this coming from and how do I find that experience at a deeper level inside myself?"

At the core of us there is one true desire which is to know ourselves as whole, complete and loving. If that is what we are desiring, the fulfillment of that desire lies at an even deeper level within. A lot of times the desire gets turned outward rather than deeper inward. Some people project their core desire onto the substance or behavior that is going to bring them some momentary pleasure. This projection creates a distortion of our core desire.

Every human being has this one true desire at the center of their being, and then every other desire is a manifestation of that one true desire. Some people get to the precipice of that one core desire and say, "Okay, now I am going to try to find my enlightenment internally." Then when they feel that core desire, it feels like an emptiness or that something is missing. However, that is the experience to stay with. That is the portal that you need to go through.

When we talk about desire, there is a difference in Eastern and Western religious philosophy. When the Buddhists say desire is the cause of suffering, it is not really desire per se. They are more-so talking about craving and grasping for things outside of ourself, whereas the West will include desire. Western mystical traditions, such as Sufi or Mystical Christianity, will see it more as a yearning of the heart. That is a core experience.

If the desire is too painful, some people externalize again and again. They do not want to feel their desire. It is the last thing they want to feel because it feels as if they are missing that which they desire. The practice is to sit in the desire itself without trying to fill it up and eventually getting to the core desire as its own experience.

If you sit with your desire, it feels empty and it feels that something is missing. However, with patience and courage the emptiness itself starts to open up into a spaciousness, and you realize nothing is missing. The desire is its own experience, a mystical state in and of itself. That is the way. In terms of your identity, it replaces a false grasping identity. It releases an identity of lack and leads you to trust in the center of your being, your true self.

## Exercise

Feel your heart's desire now. Sit and feel your heart's desire.

You are wanting something right now. In this now allow yourself to be in the wanting; let that be an experience in and of itself without trying to fill it up.

Then let the wanting expand through you like an achy feeling everywhere.

Every cell, every portion of your body is wanting this.

When this stops feeling empty, you'll see that the emptiness is actually full.

It is the desire itself that opens up into a spaciousness.

It doesn't make sense for the brain because the "thing" you are desiring is like the snake trying to swallow its own tail.

The thing you are desiring is the desire itself, but you might be missing that the desire itself has a spaciousness to it—its own experience.

This practice is useful so you can better understand desire, especially if you have experienced a strong desire for something and then got it and still did not feel fulfilled.

A "thing" will never fill you up because there is only one true desire. It is what everybody most deeply wants. You can coat it in different ways for different people—for one person it is God, for another person it is to know themselves, and for yet another it is to know love.

Whatever language you use, at the center of your being is that desire to know your wholeness, completeness and oneness. If you sit in that without trying to fill that up or do anything with it, that is enough.

When you notice the empty space itself and allow it to be there and to expand, this is your mountaintop. When you are able to sit in that space without trying to do anything with it, it has its own intelligence. This state becomes your inner guide.

This last section went deep into the topic of addictions and how to use them as an opportunity for awakening. A little reminder to keep it light and not get too heavy with this exploration. It's important because we're going to continue exploring some more types of obstacles and we want the exploration to be useful.

Much of the time we are aware of whatever obstacles we are dealing with. But there exists another class of obstacles that tend to operate outside of awareness. Because these obstacle patterns are unconscious, it makes them more difficult to identify and transform, thus we call them tenacious. Let's take a look at some examples.

## Examples of Tenacious Hidden Obstacles

What follows are a few examples of hidden obstacles. A lot of the deeper patterns are designed so that accessing them is difficult mostly because we do not know what is going on in the unconscious. These hidden obstacles are designed to be that way. They are also designed for one reason or another to not change and to remain lodged in place.

When this occurs, it is an indication of unconscious attachments—usually something from childhood that is highly valued even if it is painful. We have pulled out some key obstacles that I have encountered frequently in my practice and that usually are not addressed in mainstream literature. They are hidden shame, seeking validation and double binds.

## Working with Hidden Shame

> *"The difference between guilt and shame is very clear–in theory. We feel guilty for what we do. We feel shame for what we are."*
> ~Lewis B. Smedes

Shame is tricky because it often covers and hides the self. It also tends to remain hidden, so that people who harbor internalized shame do not even know it is an obstacle. As noted in the quote above, shame is about who and what you are—your being. Much of the time the shame is toxic because it is rooted in a lie about you. The lie says there is something inherently bad or wrong about your being. This is flat out incorrect. Remember that "you" are not the shame. It is necessary to divest the shame from the self. Separate those two out—one is toxic, the other is real.

(Please note there is also a healthy type of shame to keep us from becoming over-inflated with our own self-importance. For a good account on the difference, you can refer to John Bradshaw's book, *Healing the Shame That Binds You*.)

As an example, if someone has too much food and wine, the tendency could be to beat themselves up and say, "I am bad or wrong for that." That is toxic shame and it is a mistake. It has to be okay to have made this mistake because, if it's not, it leads you right back into the shame. There is nothing inherently bad or wrong in the behavior itself. They are making it so and tying it to their identity. Now the behavior might not be in alignment with their choices and then maybe some guilt is appropriate, but clearly not shame and frankly even the guilt is not necessary. It is not necessary if they reconnect with their choice. They can admit that, "Okay, I tripped.

I did not do so well that time. I am going to accept that." It does not have to reflect on their identity.

> MARCEY: Here's another piece to it. They had the experience of over-indulging when they had a goal not to. Then that reinforces the belief that they cannot control themself. They might think, "I am out of control." If they take that belief and reflect it back on themself, that leads to toxic false shame. They might erroneously ask, "What is wrong with me?"

> MICHAEL: In truth nothing is wrong with them. They are simply making a choice. In looking deeper, the whole thing is designed so that one will keep making the wrong choice if one has hidden shame that they are trying to get in touch with.

The shame ends up compelling their behavior. Their consciousness is trying to pull it up in order to get to the truth of their being. They keep doing it over and over and over until they finally see what it is genuinely about. They are making behavior about who they are which leads to a false self-identity. This is not necessary and internalizes a mistaken belief that something must be wrong with the self that needs correction.

What if you could look at your past mistakes, everything you have ever done wrongly or poorly, and say, "That never made me any less of a person. I am still whole and complete as I am."

There is an important dynamic to working with shame that often goes unnoticed. When someone internalizes shame, generally there is a split in the psyche that has to do with shadow work. The split creates a "good me" and a "bad me." People will tend to try to inflate or bolster the good part and suppress or deny the unacceptable or bad part. Remember, in the shadow anything that is not acceptable in our identity gets pushed out of our consciousness which perpetuates the split in the psyche. One tries to act out the good part of self and ignore the bad and it often leads to dysfunction. The bad part gets acted out unconsciously and also gets projected out onto other people. The way out of this conundrum is the realization that there is only one self. You must realize that there is nothing bad or wrong about your being even if bad behaviors have been acted out in the past. The antidote is the way of love and appreciation for who you are. You are whole and complete and there is never anything wrong with who and what you are.

## Seeking Validation

*"Because one believes in oneself, one doesn't try to convince others. Because one is content with oneself, one doesn't need others' approval. Because one accepts oneself, the whole world accepts him or her."*
–Lao Tzu

For exploring the next hidden obstacle, we must set the stage by understanding our past and our upbringing as children. When children are growing up, their first sense of identity comes from a reflection through the eyes of their parents. When a parent stares into the eyes of their child in the early stages of development, the child is getting its first sense of self. The child learns to calibrate themself from the parents. Let's explain this further with an analogy.

Imagine a scale from 0 to 10 of how alive you are. How alive are you? How awake are you? How vibrant are you?

The range is from 0 (I am pretty much walking dead) to 10 (I am fully alive, fully awake).

Let us say the parents are at a 6 and when they are looking into their baby's eyes and are doing the goo-goo-ga-ga thing. What the baby is doing is tracking its own identity. They will get that first imprint of their own aliveness as 6. They take the cues from the parent and calibrate themselves to a 6.

Now if the parent is checked out and they cannot adequately reflect back to the child, the child will remain unrecognized as an opportunity for the parent to get it right. The child is deeply wishing for the parent to reflect back to them who they know themselves to be, and they will allow no other reflections because they are waiting for the parent to do it.

Often adults who are seeking or wanting to know their worth and value will keep themselves from the experience as a retroactive way for the parent to get it right. Even though it goes back into the past, even though the opportunity is past, there continues to be a function that is seeking to be seen and heard by mom and/or dad.

It bears repeating another way. The children's first identity comes from how seen they are by their parents. If that reflection is not adequately mirrored back for the child, what occurs is that a psychological aspect of the child's existence is not validated. In order to seek affirmation, the child continues to look for that mirroring from the parent or from a surrogate parent. If it is not adequately mirrored in childhood, or worse if it is absent altogether, then the child moves into adulthood trying to get a parent to see and validate them. This can occur with the father, with the mother or with both.

The obstacle manifests when we become adults. It is a childhood program and it is the "inner child" that is seeking validation. There is a function that is still trying to get something that is not available because we are no longer children. It is a setup. Then people with this obstacle will project that childhood need for validation onto their partners, onto their families and onto other aspects of life. Overcoming this obstacle is accomplished by getting in touch with that early need. Then one needs to self-validate in the place where they needed the validation from the parent or from outside themselves.

You have to get first in touch with the lack, the feeling of not getting validated and what that is like. Then once you are in touch with that, you shift that feeling into what it is like when you self-validate—when you no longer need that external validation. Essentially, you fill the need from the inside out. At that point the validation becomes internal, and then it will free up the individual from needing it any longer.

When we talk about this as a hidden obstacle, we are talking about something deeper. The need for validation is not conscious. It is not something that most people are in touch with until they recognize it. It is at a very deep level, under the surface, in the unconscious part of our experience—this need of parental validation. Many of the obstacles' people are dealing with—for instance, self-esteem issues, power struggles or narcissism—much of the time will end up coming down to that need for validation.

It is often an unseen function and there are levels to the underlying needs. The tenacious nature of this obstacle is because some people do not know they are seeking validation. The person may not know that they were not adequately validated as a child. Yet the function in their psyche remains in effect.

The need is sending out a beacon, waiting for a response and not getting one, so it keeps sending out a beacon in hopes that something outside them will reset that circuit. The beacon is saying, "Please see me! Please see me!" or "Please hear me!" and not getting a response, so it is not getting reset.

This is different than wanting an opinion validated. It is going to show up very differently because people are not in touch with the fact that they are needing this childhood validation.

Is this common?

It can be because of the lack of consciousness in parenting. It is not abuse, but more often the parents' attention is going other places. The unaware parent does not notice the need in their child. If parents could be more conscious, they would give pure undivided attention to their children. This is the function we call mirroring. Once mirroring is given at any stage, human beings start to feel seen and heard.

Mirroring goes to the primitive part of our brain and validates us at that level. It is below the threshold of our everyday thought. It is the memory of one's inner child that needs the validation. Problems arise when the adult goes about unconsciously seeking this validation. That is when this becomes an issue. The mirror was originally not available to them in the past and they are still trying to get it.

In working with this obstacle, you have to go into the past and bring your child self the recognition it needs. A lot of times people will not do it because they want the parent to get it right in the memory. They want to retroactively try to make different facts happen in the past, but that can't happen. They end up not moving toward resolution because they want that validation only from the parents. You have to go back into the memory, into the past, as early as possible (optimally in memories from the first five years of life) and get in touch with the relationship with parents. What was or was not happening at that time in your life?

There is another hidden dimension of this. By remaining wounded by the parents' lack of attention, one preserves the only evidence that the parents did anything wrong. If one heals the wound, it lets the parents off the hook. If one is trying to stick it to or punish their parents for their lack of parenting, they need to hold on to the wound as the only evidence of that lack. Keep in mind this is usually an unconscious process—someone would not easily admit that they want their parents to continue to pay the price for their bad childhood.

It is not going to be this way across the board for everyone, so you have to test and check for yourself. Are these aspects in effect or not?

Is there a component of forgiveness around your upbring when you go back and are able to work with childhood memories?

Of course. However, forgiveness may not be the most useful piece to get a pattern to shift. What if the parents did nothing wrong? Then there is no need for forgiveness. It could have been a consequence of them not having enough bandwidth to pay attention to the child.

Rather than forgiveness I would ask, "What is it like if you had the attention you wanted as a child? How would that have affected how you feel about yourself?" That is different than forgiveness. Forgiveness is definitely part of our awakening, but I always find forgiveness a little bit tricky because it implies someone else's wrongdoing. In some cases, there are real wrongs done to us—for instance, when abuse occurs. However, sometime people can perceive being wronged when that is not what is occurring.

MARCEY: Are you saying it may be an outcome to have forgiven someone, but it is not the method to change the pattern itself?

MICHAEL: Correct. You can forgive them and the pattern could be running in your neurology. The tape is running, and buttons are still getting pushed that trigger the program.

MARCEY: We used a parenting coach when our kids were little, and I remember the most important thing she had said is, the primary thing your kids want from you as a parent is connection.

MICHAEL: How do you know when you have connection?

MARCEY: Part of it is easy stuff, for example, having a conversation, playing games without distraction, being present with them, being a good listener, hearing what they are saying, making eye contact and validating what they say when they express themselves. There was a heart connection also. Sometimes I would have to stop what I was doing (usually half-listening), then feel or visualize my heart being open. Then I could feel the connection, and they let their guard down and opened up in a different way. Also, you do not have an agenda when talking to them.

What would it be like to have been seen as a child? If parents could look in the eyes of their children and tell them, "You are whole, complete and wonderful as you are" and the parent knows that and experiences that in themselves as well. Then the children are going to get that.

Let us say the parent is checked out or stressed out. When their attention is going to different places, the child is still trying to get that parental reflection. They end up seeking it over and over... and as they grow into adulthood if that is not dealt with it, it becomes an overlay for all of life. They project the unmet need outward and end up experiencing their life as the parent who did not validate them. They don't get recognized by the world around them.

It is the wanting to be seen and heard: "Do I really exist?" or "Do I exist as a fully awake, alive human being?" Are you getting your sense of self from your upbringing or from your true identity?

MARCEY: I have heard people talk often about trying to fill the need of validation from their parents in unusual ways, through mentors, bosses, or leaders whom they see unconsciously as a father or mother figure.

MICHAEL: It happens, such as in marriages where we end up marrying our parents' replacement (in an odd way). We are trying to get re-parented properly. It wreaks havoc on the marriage because that is inappropriate to ask that of our partner.

Life itself can operate as one big parent figure. One can project that parent figure onto life, and then life treats them the same way that the parent did. If one is not in touch with the validation needs left by their parents, they could be constantly looking for mommy and daddy to tell them that they are okay and constantly projecting that need onto life.

If this dynamic applies to you, once you get through this you can begin to self-validate. Self-validation is where you no longer need externalized validation. You do not need anyone to behave in any way to know you are okay.

It is like a ping process; when you put out a ping, you want a response. People put pings out and expect a response. However, if your parents did not respond to you, then whenever you put out a ping, nothing came back. That is where the seeking comes from. The searching for validation comes in because you are not getting life to reflect back who you want to be seen as.

The key to shifting this is understanding the True Self/False Self. You can refer back to this section in Part One if you need a refresh on the tool.

Once you get to your true self-identity, you no longer need validation as you continually self-validate from within. Then once you know you are worth it, the ping is going to send back the kind of response you want. Everything in that externalizing links up with the interior. That is when the inner and the outer reflect each other in a wonderful way.

## Double Binds

Double binds are a particularly tenacious pattern. This is when you are having an experience and you want to move out of it. When you start to move out of it, you move to another negative experience that you also want to move out of. That one makes you move back toward the original negative one and you end up bouncing between two negatives. You get stuck trying to escape the negative and the solution is always the other negative pole. You never get to a real solution because you bounce between two negative outcomes. At that point the whole unworkable dynamic must be shut out of consciousness. The key to working with this type of patten is to reference a third state, a completely new state of affairs that does not involve trying to escape either of the previous unworkable solutions.

Here's an example. I had a client who was a type A personality, but suffered anxiety from the pressure they constantly put on themselves to perform at such a high level. They were very successful in their career, but when they tried to slow down and take a break, they would be confronted with a deep fear of failure rooted in a hidden low self-esteem from past mistakes. They had developed the successful behavior as a way to counter their low self-esteem. And it worked.

The problem was now they were caught between the two poles of pressure to perform and fear of crashing into low self-esteem. The way to resolution was in getting them in touch with their inherent value even in the light of past failures and mistakes. When they could reference that, the pressure subsided and they could begin to perform by choice rather than by compulsion. They could begin to see a different way.

By now you should have an understanding of different types of obstacles and how they get created neurologically in your brain (remember, it is sensory based—VAKOG). Now onto my favorite part of the process, transformation and how to get the changes you want!

# CHAPTER 13

▲ ▲ ▲

# Tools for Transforming
# Obstacles into New Experiences

*"We delight in the beauty of the butterfly, but rarely admit the
changes it has gone through to achieve that beauty."*
~Maya Angelou

We are going to cover several tools in the next chapter. Not every tool is effective for every pattern you wish to shift. Use a tool if it works, or keep exploring if the tool doesn't seem to function for you.

## Memories as Filters for Our Experiences

How do your memories play into your experiences and why is this important to understand?

Memory is a record of everything you have experienced in your life. Memories, and most especially their emotional impact, operate as filtering mechanisms. Everything comes in through your senses, but before you become aware of it, before it gets to the neo-cortex, it gets fed through your memories which operate as filters from your past.

There is a system in the brain called the reticular activating system. In this part of your brain the filters can make things appear differently than they actually are. You can misperceive situations

> ## 🔑 KEY CONCEPT
>
> *There are filtering systems in your brain that make things seem different than they actually are because they are reinterpreting what is happening through filters created from the past.*

because, in these situations you are not seeing things as they are, but seeing a re-interpretation based on your filtering from the past.

The filtering causes you to see what you want and need to see. It is very powerful because it can filter out evidence of goodness in your life. You could filter out negative aspects, but you could also filter out positive aspects of what is happening.

For instance, consider when someone falsely believes they are unloved by other people. If that is their belief, then the evidence of how they are loved and where there is love in their life will be filtered out. The brain will do a delete on the actual evidence because the "I am unloved" belief filtering is in operation.

Imagine it like a set of colored lenses that you look through. If your lens is blue, then everything in life is going to look blue. If your filters are red, then everything in life is going to look red. What would happen if you were able to look through clear filters?

What does your life look like when you are not coloring your present based on your past experiences? Life is more "as it is" versus as you "want it to be" or "hope it to be."

> MARCEY: Is that even achievable? For me it feels like I am fighting my brain when I try to see things as they are and not as I interpret them from my perspective.

> MICHAEL: That is the tendency of the mind. Your filters are operating and the mind tries to grasp at clarity. Some people get to a clear mind by sitting for long periods in meditation and letting the mind calm down.

What if you could take your reactions out of it and noticing clearly what is happening? What would it be like if momentarily you removed yourself out of the equation? Along with removing any judgment as well. For example, you could simply notice someone else's reaction without having to have a reaction to their reaction.

You could also apply that to yourself as well. The objective observer helps you with this. For a moment imagine what it would be like to have no attachment or judgment about yourself or anything you experience.

The next section gives a way to begin to uncover some of these types of memories.

## Eye Accessing and Accessing Core Imprints

Eye accessing is the premier tool for getting to unconscious content. When you process information, your eyes will track the processing. When you are running sense data in your mind (those Vs, As, and Ks), your eyes are going to be moving to different locations as you get different data. The eye movements track the information you process.

Typically, when your eyes are above the line of the ear, you are in the visual range and are processing pictures. When eyes are moving around the ear level, you are processing more auditory content. When looking down, you tend to process more feelings and internal self-talk or internal dialogue.

The access is when you hit a pain point or a memory that is informing a particular experience. Notice where you are looking when you have a particular experience. A lot of times the access happens in the first half-second of running a program, so be patient with yourself when exploring this. It can be challenging using this tool because it is very difficult to observe your own unconscious. It helps to have someone watch you and give feedback about what they notice.

Where do your eyes move? What are you looking at in your mind's eye (or listening to in your mind's ear) when your eyes are at a certain location (relative to the program you are trying to shift)?

When we are talking about transformation, the core imprints are the more impactful ones that are going to inform an obstacle. Usually, there is a core imprint, a trauma from the past, a painful event, anything that happened that made an impact in the early years. The brain continues to process that by referencing the memory and any pain of it. Generally, with eye accessing you can get to some of these core imprints.

How does this work?

You are going to be looking for the access that informs the problem state or the current state you are intending to shift. It will be a very repeatable, very consistent experience. Every time you reference or load up the program that is getting in the way, your eyes will do the same sequential movement. Look at the first step in that sequence. What are you looking at or listening to that gives rise to a particular feeling?

That is going to happen very quickly, normally in fractions of a second. Again, be patient if you are working with this tool and ask someone to observe you and to give feedback for what they notice.

Once you are aware of an access, what is a good way to shift it? This question brings us to our next tool in transforming obstacles—time traveling.

## Time Traveling to Revise Past Patterns and Gain Future Insights

Time traveling is a way to explore bringing your resources from the present into a memory structure from the past, so that the "you"

> ### 🔑 KEY CONCEPT
>
> *Time traveling is a way to bring your current wisdom and self to your past, as a way to inform or reassure your younger self. This process can be transformational.*

in the past is a healthy functional "you" and is better able to support the outcome in the present that you want.

When you experience transformational work, a good portion of the time is spent unpacking an obstacle in order to get to the access (the informing memory). The actual change is a fairly easy thing once you have the access. You might spend a lot of time trying to find the access, but once you have it then you have the key to transformation.

> MARCEY: This reminds me of the point that your brain does not necessarily know (or can distinguish) between things that happened in real time versus history or in your imagination.

> MICHAEL: Yes, remember there are filtering mechanisms that filter through your memory banks. They filter based on the past and thus filter how the present looks. When you travel back to the past and adjust the filters (the memories and how they are processed), it changes how the present looks.

That is what we mean by time travel. A different way of saying that is bringing resources from the present into the past or resources from the future into the present. In the first scenario where you are going into the past, it is working with memories. In the second scenario where you are going into the future, it is working with imagination.

You could imagine doing a guided meditation, where you visit yourself when you are older and listen to that wise version of yourself—and ask them what you need to know. It is a way of tricking the brain to get access to information. It is a trick, but it works.

> MARCEY: That is pretty amazing. I have done exercises in visualizing myself in what I think is perfect health, in a different physical body that looks different, as an example. I have done that and have been able to connect, but I like the thought of using your imagination to bring wisdom to inform what your older self would be like. What would this future "you" say to yourself now?

> MICHAEL: Here's a way to enhance the effect even more. When you are in a deeper state, more of a meditative state, the exercise will have more impact. If you are doing it in your normal thought processes, it may not bear that much fruit. But when you are in a deeper trance state, and then you do these imaginations, some especially powerful information sometimes comes through.

> MARCEY: Is it important to "feel the feelings" or feel these thoughts in our body?

> MICHAEL: Yes, unless it is a trauma from the past. That can be part of the problem—that one gets too steeped in it and too stuck in the feelings of it. In that case it helps to get out of the feelings in order to get a break. If you are stuck in a filter, then everything's going to be processing through that filter.

It is not always about feeling the feelings, but about the context. There are times when you need to feel the feelings and be associated into a memory. Then there are times when you need to get some distance from an experience and have some perspective on it by using your objective observer.

> MARCEY: Are there times when you have worked with clients and they are unwilling to time travel and there is some resistance to revising those patterns?

> MICHAEL: Yes, and resistance is not a problem. Resistance usually means the person is protecting the memory, even if it is painful, or that their system is trying to keep them safe. A lot of times you can pace the resistance. You can try something different, a different exercise.

Sometimes if they are extremely resistant, I stop and say, "Okay, you are too strong and powerful in your resistance for me to guide you to a breakthrough here." Rather than battle with the person you let them win. Consciously, they want the breakthrough but unconsciously they do not. This technique is to bring the person to their unconscious truth. Then they may say that they really do want the breakthrough. It is important to understand someone's hidden power stance. They can be lodged and stuck in a state where they are using their power to maintain the state even though it is limiting for them. Their power is going on behind the scenes to keep the thing in place, and they are being very powerful about the thing that is holding them back.

Usually when we get resistance it is because of that power; their power is wrapped up in maintaining the state. Yet feeling unsafe can also cause someone to feel resistance.

The next tool in working with transformation is working with the Archetypes. We are discussing them at this stage because of their depth and impact in the human experience. Also, much of the time the archetypal themes remain unconscious and contain hidden aspects that can help transform experience through greater awareness.

## Working with Archetypes, Energies and Shadow Work

Archetypes are from the work of Carl Jung. Archetypes are larger life themes with their own energy. They reside in the collective unconscious of all humanity throughout all time...thus they have energy and power to them. When we say working with archetypes and energies, they are very close to the same thing. The archetypes are known by their energy.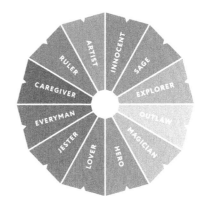

Here are some examples: mother is an archetype, the hero is an archetype, the monk is an archetype. Any role we play can be an archetype. Problems begin to occur when people get identified with the archetype. As an example, many women get identified with the role of mother and it feeds them. It has energy and it gives them energy. The problem is if you get too identified with the archetype, it can possess you, because archetypes have their own consciousness.

If we look at someone who is in the hero archetype, and that archetype starts to take over, they are not allowed to have a human experience at that point; they have to constantly be a hero. Perfectionism might set in. It can be great to work with the hero archetype, but you do not want to get identified with any of these archetypal roles. Some of them are very powerful, and some of them can be very negative as well. The villain is an archetype. The bully is an archetype.

> MARCEY: When kids move out of the house, a lot of parents have to stop and figure out who they are because of the connection to the parenting role for so long.

> MICHAEL: That is because the archetype is feeding you through the energy of that role and it is supposed to. However, at some point it runs its course. For me the adventurer is a big archetype. It has energy. When I go out on an adventure, I get this energy because the archetype is feeding me energy. But if I get too much in

the adventurer role, I end up not getting much done. Too much adventure and maybe I would have never written this book.

You have to keep your archetypes in check. You can work with them, but as one of my guides told me, "You do not want to mainline them." You do not want to get overly identified with any archetype. There are whole books written on archetypes alone, so we will not go into it too deeply here. Notice that at a very deep level within you, when you are getting deep into the unconscious by seeing bigger themes and life patterns, archetypes are going to come into play.

> MARCEY: When working archetypes (and energies), is part of this understanding which archetype or roles you have as a useful tool? What do you mean by working with our archetypes?

> MICHAEL: I mean noticing the bigger theme you are playing out in your life. As an example, the most common archetype in America is the hero. Many of us want to be the hero, to rush in and save the day. There is also the rugged cowboy (cowboy is an archetype) conquering the next frontier. In working with any archetype, it is about getting in touch with the energy of it. There is a quantum of energy within each archetype.

They provide energy and they are very powerful. If you are not in touch with that energy, it can possess you. What I am talking about when I say "working with it" is mostly being aware of it and noticing the energy of it. Don't let those energies run you.

- Do you identify with any of the archetype roles?
- Are you getting overly attached to the energy an archetype is providing you?
- Can you enjoy the energy going through the experience of it without getting identified with it?

You can play out the hero, but that does not mean you have to be the hero. You can play out the adventurer, but as soon as you become overly identified and need to be the adventurer twenty-four hours a day, seven days a week, it does not leave the door open for other experiences. The priest is an archetype. The CEO is an archetype. The healer is an archetype.

Some of the negative archetypes could be the manipulator. The thief could be an archetype.

**KEY CONCEPT**

*In Jungian psychology archetypes represent universal patterns and images that are part of the collective unconscious. Jung believed that we inherit these archetypes much in the way we inherit instinctive patterns of behavior. Begin to see the themes that come about in your life.*

They are roles. What if one is possessed by the thief archetype? Are they compelled to steal?

Could the archetypes that you work with change?

Yes, and they will. They will typically change throughout the chapters of your life. Some can be with us the whole of our life. As an example, let's look at the monk archetype. They commit their life to being a monk—that is an archetype and it provides them energy. But somewhere down the road on their journey, they have to find their experience beyond being a monk. Let's say after twenty years of being a monk, the monk archetype may start to run out of juice. Then what happens?

Especially if they still want to live out the life. They have to find something else to feed them. The old energy is not going to work anymore.

The lover is an archetype that can be very compelling. The king and the queen are big archetypes. Others are the magician, the warrior. Wonder Woman is an archetype. The warrior is very powerful because that gives one the energy to fight. But what if someone is possessed by the warrior? They may feel righteousness and behave aggressively. You do not want the archetype to control you. You want to use it, but do not let it use you.

Could you use the energy of an archetype for good?

Absolutely. They are natural. As an example, how about if you are in the mother archetype. It is natural for you and that is what gives you a lot of the energy to do what you need to do as a mother. The problem is, as you said, when your kids move out and if you have been overly identified with the role of mother, then you don't know who are you. Then you have to go through the process of rediscovering your identity. After the kids move out, you can have another archetype feed you for a while, but it may not have the same impact.

From the wise old sage to the jester or fool, begin to see the themes that come about in your life.

In this chapter we have explored some powerful tools for transforming obstacles, but the toolbox goes far beyond what we have shared. The real key is to find the transformative tools that work best for you. There are many modalities and ways to live this transformative lifestyle. Find your own way and find what works best for you to get the results you want.

We have now reached a turning point in this journey. We are beginning to get beyond the concept of the self. Much of the time as individuals, we are influenced by factors outside of our awareness that are greater than us. Yet often the influences and how they affect us can remain unconscious. The following chapter is for becoming aware of these effects and serves as a primer for the final part of this book.

# CHAPTER 14

▲ ▲ ▲

# The Beginning of Self-Transcendence

## Systems Thinking

Everything up until this point is about you as an individual. As we progress, we want to introduce a concept of systemic influences, or ways that the individual is influenced outside of their awareness by systems that they are a part of. Systems are greater than us as individuals and have powerful sway that often goes unnoticed.

In *The Art of Systems Thinking* by O'Conner and McDermott, they define systems and define emergent properties within a system. A system is an entity that maintains its existence and functions as a whole through the interaction of its parts. Some of you might find it helpful to understand a bit about systems in general. Here are some key summary points:

> ▷ A system contains interconnecting parts that function as a whole.

> ▷ The system changes if you take away or add more parts. If you cut a system in half, you do not get two smaller systems, but a damaged system that will probably not function.

> ▷ The arrangement of the parts is crucial.

> ▷ The parts are connected and work together.

> ▷ The system's behavior depends on the total structure—change the structure and the behavior changes.

> ▷ Emergent properties are properties found in the system that are not found in the parts.

While this is a broad overview of systems, systems are typically more complex. In The *Inside Guide* our focus is on systems that aid in transformation. Thus, we are going to focus on specific systems

177

and start with the most impactful for any human being—the family system.

## The Genetics of your Family System/Ancestral influences

The most important system to understand, the one with the biggest impact on your life, is the family system. The family system is an energy field within and around you. It is like a bubble you are inside of without realizing it.

Imagine if you will, that all the information for your entire history is within you. Somehow woven into your DNA along with your genetic coding is all the emotional and painful information of your past, but even more of your entire lineage. All the things that your family of origin held as valuable, sacred, taboo, important, etc. are held in an energy field around you that obligates and sways you away from your own free will—away from the unique life you were born to lead.

In order to work with this, you have to open up to your system itself—almost sensing into this unseen energy field. How you do that is by first having the frame of reference for it and then cultivating a part of yourself that is sensitive to that level of our existence as human beings. It also takes practice. As you develop a framework for this internally, expect that something is going to come up, and that something is going to be brought to the surface. It is a sensing of sorts. You sense the bigger field around each of us (I recognize this is somewhat abstract). There is a sense within you that can begin to pick up on the field itself.

How can we learn more about this system, this energy field? If this identity is unconscious, can we examine it ourselves or does that have to be done with a professional?

Both of course. As I said in the beginning, we need others to help us see our blind spots. It is also important to work on your own as well. Here are some helpful questions for self-exploration:

- How does it benefit your family of origin to maintain any self-limiting experiences you might be stuck in?
- Whom are you being loyal to by maintaining these types of experiences?
- Can you imagine any places in your life where you are living

out the unlived life of your parents?

This whole concept comes out of the work of Bert Hellinger, a German psychotherapist. He developed family systems and family constellations as a means for healing people. A big part of his work is understanding the dictates of the conscience. The conscience has levels to it that operate hierarchically—the personal, the family and the collective. The study is deeply intensive, and as an introduction we will address the personal and family conscience and their drivers of guilt and innocence.

There is a phrase we used in training that says, "In a family of thieves the child who does not steal is the guilty one." If a family has a code that dictates the members must be thieves and then one child says, "No, I am not going to steal", then that child is doing the right thing. The child is innocent on the personal level, but guilty on the family level by breaking the family rule. Usually, the child is compelled more by the family level.

It is not only breaking family rules; it may also come with the fear of being an outcast. There are multiple arms to these things. One arm is the fear of being an outcast and along with that the fear of survival. It is not only painful; it also deeply affects survival and identity. When someone erroneously believes they do not belong anymore, it can also lead to hidden fear, guilt and shame.

The way you rectify this is by first understanding that you can never be cast out of your family, even if you were physically cast out. You are and always will be a member of your family system; nothing can change that. But how you belong makes all the difference in the world.

If you switch your belonging to the genetics, you belong and will always belong because you are the daughter or son of your parents. This is factual. Your belonging is not determined by how much family pain you have or how much you get wrapped up in family matters. This understanding is how we deal with the fear of being an outcast. You can never be cast out.

## The Spectrum of the Family System

A lot of the tenacious obstacles that are resistant to change get lodged in place. They are lodged on one end by fear and survival—that primal fight, flight, freeze response. On the other end of the spectrum, on the opposite end from fear, there is love. When fear and love work together, the resistance to change becomes very strong. A big part that often goes unnoticed is that love can operate as an unconscious driver which keeps us stuck.

Love in Family Systems generally says, "I will do my part to try to take as much pain as possible away from my family." I love them that much. The child gets caught trying to live out the hero or savior archetypes and possibly also the martyr or the victim. Whatever is not being addressed in the system or whatever needs healing, the child will tend to tap into and then take that on as their own mission in life. It is hard to unravel because a lot of times there are positive benefits to maintaining this grandiose mission.

## How is it actually working?

If you have this pain, you can get to work on it. You can attempt to solve it and then bring that solution back to the family, and become the hero of the family. You could be a hero—that is a potential that could make the pain worthwhile. You could get to wear your halo very straight in your angelic archetype. However, none of this is going to work because you are trying to fix something that is not yours to fix. What keeps one stuck is the secondary gain—the hope that it could succeed.

The child wants to be the hero and wants to save the family. But that child never gets to that experience because the thing they have taken to solve on behalf of the family is an unsolvable problem. That is an example of one dynamic you need to look at in these unconscious drivers.

This can spin in different ways and that is what is tricky when you are unraveling and unpacking these dynamics. This whole line of questioning and the concepts it reveals are what people can be afraid of. If you break the rules by making something conscious, do you risk rejection by your family? Have you been rejected for living your authentic self, specifically rejected by your family of origin? That experience can be scary and painful. Scary because there can be a built-in sense of loyalty and expectations when you are part of a family. With this unit that raised you, if being authentic means going against the family dynamics, it may feel disloyal.

Let's take a look at a couple of examples:

Say I am working with a woman and she is having a painful experience such as a body image issue. With some unpacking and digging we see it originated in her upbringing. Maybe we notice the same pattern in one of her parents. We see this is not her issue, but in fact her mother's. Now we can understand why she became invested in the pattern. As a child and an adult, this client loves her mother. She is trying to get a connection with her mother to have a better experience by taking on the problem on her mother's behalf. Now we see the woman is caught in a web of her own childhood making. She either has the pain, and feels loving and loyal, and maintains her childhood innocence; or she lets go of it and then feels guilty.

In a second scenario, a man acts cold and stoic to appease his cold stoic father... who probably acted cold and stoic to appease his cold and stoic father. This is a generational pattern passed from ancestors to their descendants. The son feels angry with his father, but propagates the behavior out of loyalty. By unconsciously taking on the issue, he can hope to work it out on his father's behalf. When the man realizes that his father was in the same boat and that the issue was never his, he can connect to the love that caused him to take on the issue. Over time he learns to relate to his father in a new way.

## A Real Family System Example

CLIENT: I had a big shift over the weekend about my physical health. During some quiet time of reflection, I realized that I have abused my body with food because I felt that "I am damned if I do, damned if I don't." If I got healthy, then I am disloyal to this family because of their perspective on healthy fit people. If you are healthy, skinny, worked out, etc., then you were also probably egotistical and selfish. To be self-less you would spend time to take care of others and not yourself. There hasn't been a way to take care of ourselves in a way that does not seem selfish.

MICHAEL: Taking care of yourself is going to be selfish. It is going to create guilt. It is how to reprogram those experiences, so you do not have to accept the family rules. If something is authentic and you bump up against the system, then that system has sway over you until you are no longer affected by it. Again, you will always be a part of the system, but it does not have to influence you with its rules. It is even possible for families to unconsciously lie to their members as a way to keep everyone in line.

In my own life I am part of a very dysfunctional family system. I do not talk to some of my siblings anymore because it is not healthy for me. However, I am connected to them. I am their brother and I always will be. I am a part of the family—they are a part of the family. We will always be connected. Now I love them from a distance. I am guilty of breaking the dysfunctional rules, yet now I am no longer swayed by the dynamics I grew up in.

CLIENT: That is the empowering part, when it is possible to be around or be in a family, and authentically be yourself while letting those around you authentically be themselves. Sometimes that means enforcing boundaries.

MICHAEL: One aspect of what empowerment means to me is when I can be who I am while letting others be who they are. Dysfunctional families try to make you feel guilty in order to get you back in the cage metaphorically speaking. The game I like in describing this is Whack-a-Mole. Whack-a-Mole is where the mole comes up in different places and you try to whack it down. That is what dysfunctional systems try to do. Every time someone pops up, the system tries to whack them down. There is a hidden jealousy. Those who are caught by the system ask, "Who are you to have a wonderful life while we are still suffering?"

## Healthy vs. Toxic Guilt

There is a type of guilt we need to bear with dignity. Thus it is useful to make a distinction between the toxic kind of guilt which keeps you stuck in the past, and a healthy guilt which breaks you free.

In toxic guilt, family systems use manipulation as one of the tactics to keep the members in line. You see it in other systems such as corporate environments, spiritual groups, clubs, affiliations, etc. Every system has its way of trying to control its members.

Healthy guilt says, "Yes, I am guilty of no longer being swayed by the systems I am part of. I am the one who is breaking free, and that makes me guilty." Children are innocent and one way they maintain this innocence into adulthood is by maintaining a childhood stance. It is as if they're saying, "It is okay. I am going to do it. I have always done it. I am going to continue to play my family role." How sweet and innocent.

You can break out and say, "You know what? I am not doing that anymore. I am going to be the guilty one if I do that, but it is a dignified guilt."

Here's a quick inquiry:

*Notice what is it like when you're no longer guilty.*

*Notice these feelings.*

*Notice what it is like when you are also no longer innocent.*

*Notice these feelings.*

*Now notice the two together: not guilty and not innocent!*

This is an opportunity for awakening. You are not innocent anymore. Stop playing that game. Stop playing the child. Awaken to the mature and dignified adult guilt. Step into it to say, "I am awake. That makes me guilty. The rest of my family might be asleep and they're going to try to keep me back in that sleep. I am not going there anymore."

Now let's take another leap in consciousness to understanding and working with evolutionary influences.

## Evolutionary Influences

When we discussed family systems, we saw that your history goes beyond the personal by genetically recording your ancestry as well. When you are ready to go beyond your ancestry, you can start to look at evolutionary influences. These are the issues and themes that would be common to all human beings in general. Issues such as violence, abuse and deception have been part of humanity's dysfunction through time. This is what we mean by evolutionary influences.

It is also the unresolved history of the human race overall. If you look through history, there are ways in which humanity has struggled to survive. Is there enough food? Enough water? Is the other tribe going to attack us? These things that you imagine earlier people going through since the start of the species are part of you. You are influenced by these factors. As one example, there was a time in history when if you were from a different tribe, you were a threat and had to be killed. That violence is in each of us in a deep level of our collective shadow. Maybe you think this would not affect you and that you cannot be provoked at that level. It may have to be a very stressful threatening situation in order for that to get provoked, but it is still in there in potential.

> ### 🔑 KEY CONCEPT
>
> *Evolutionary influences are typically unconscious, but we can learn to be aware of them and the influence they may have in our lives.*

As an individual, how are you affected by these collective issues? Can you challenge any of your own violent or hurtful impulses?

There is a progression in our development as human beings. This progression would be first your individual or personal issues, then your family's history, then the evolutionary influences. You can see this progression…

INDIVIDUAL          ANCESTRAL          EVOLUTIONARY

The same way that you have been influenced by unresolved ancestral factors, you are also influenced by the human race and what human beings have experienced through time. Think of the wars, the violence and the atrocities that have occurred in our collective past. I believe there is a record this in our DNA and that we are somehow connected to it.

I do not think I would have been in touch with this understanding until my martial arts practice. It got me in touch with some very violent impulses within myself which I might not have noticed. Once I noticed those, it gave me more choice around it. I did not have to act out violence and I could channel that energy into positive outcomes. In order to free ourselves from violence, we have to notice our own tendency for violence (and any codependent relationships with violence in others).

I think overcoming violence is a very important factor in the evolution of the human race. Violence, murder, rape, abuse, etc.— these are things that have happened through time, and it is not going to benefit us moving forward to be caught in those. One of the biggest themes of that is the cycle of abuse and victimization. It is a repeating cycle that happens not only in families, but is more and more running rampant through our society these days.

Ask yourself, "How am I being affected by things outside of my awareness, the things every human being ought to face and challenge?" It could be food issues as another example. When you are challenging food issues, you are also up against the billions of people, since the start of the human race, who have starved. How deep do you take it? Typically, in our western society there is plenty of food. Consider that nowadays food is very accessible, but there were times in history, and in certain places, where that was not the case. Even today, for billions there are issues about getting enough to eat. We are not separate from that.

We will explore this more in the Part Three, but when you are connected to everyone else, you cannot ignore those issues. You can develop empathy for what it is like for someone to starve even though you might not have starved yourself.

These systemic influences are typically unconscious. They are operating outside of your awareness until you notice their effects and free yourself from any negative influences they might create.

> MARCEY: I did not completely understand the concept of maternal instinct, or how strong my maternal instinct was until I had a child. Going through my life, I was not sure if I wanted to have kids. Then when I had my first son, I felt this immediate maternal instinct that felt as if it took over my rational brain, who I thought I was. It was almost overwhelming. It felt as if it was consuming me

which triggered anxiety, because the feeling of protecting this little thing outside of myself was a lot. I would give up everything for this other being. I had been a career minded, working person my whole life. My focus was on achievement, being independent, but in an instant, I felt a role change. The minute I had this child, that was it. I knew it was something evolutionary, something instinctive. I knew it was not just another side of myself; it felt bigger than me, my personality, my experiences. It is as though this was stored in my DNA and was finally stirred awake.

MICHAEL: These instincts are always under the threshold of awareness. Some are useful and some are not in terms of your transformation and humanity's evolution. What affects most people negatively is the violent impulse, the violent instinct. Please be aware of any tendencies toward violence and practice feeling safe in your body. Peace must first happen within you if we want it for our planet.

## The Love-Soul Model

The love-soul model is similar to the family systems model but looks more at love itself as kind of an "over soul" for each of us.

When we use the word soul, we want to be careful because it has religious implications for a lot of people. Here we are using soul and love interchangeably. It is the part of your experience that allows everything that is occurring. It says that everything that is happening in your life—good, bad and indifferent—is included in the soul. It is what you are here to work out in life.

This soul or love is the backdrop that allows you to have your human experiences. Love has a certain consciousness to it, and it wants inclusion. It wants all the members of your family to be acknowledged and to be included in the overall system. It says everyone belongs in a family. You may want to create physical boundaries

> ⚷ **KEY CONCEPT**
>
> *The love-soul model is not romantic or emotional love; it is a state of being.*

with family members but the model is about acknowledging the inclusion of everyone on the level of soul. Taken at a bigger level, we could say everyone belongs here on planet earth. Everyone that is incarnated here belongs here. Everyone is included with no exceptions.

If you had a dimension to yourself that allowed all of your experiences, and loved yourself and others no matter what, what would that be like? Imagine what it is like for you to get in touch with that?

There is nothing to do in working with this model. This is an issue for some people. In this model, the soul model, it is less about doing and is much more about being. Some people think everything has to be action oriented, that they have to do something. This is not always the case. Sometimes it is about doing nothing. It is an awareness which supports more noticing and allowing.

> MARCEY: That sounds good in theory, but practically it seems like I live on one side or the other. I feel frustration with the people around me (for instance, when the kids come home, throw their stuff down and make a mess) or I feel in a peaceful Zen space.

> MICHAEL: On one end you have your primal neurology, and on the other end you have the soul. Imagine they are two ends of the spectrum from complete physiology to completely not physical.

> MARCEY: It sometimes feels like a tug-of-war between the sides. There are times when I could be in that loving-full-soul, full-body connection place, or I am in my neurology and my patterns and habits. This is being on the mountaintop or fighting it out in the village.

> MICHAEL: They are not separate. The loving place contains your habits and patterns; it holds them all. It is the consciousness that says these are okay even if they remain as obstacles.

There are times when one says, "No, I do not want this. I know this experience and I don't want it." Yet from the soul perspective the soul does not care. The soul says, "Have it. That is your experience and it is okay even if you are in pain." The human part of you cares if you are in pain. The soul says anything that is occurring is acknowledged and included. It is really love.

This love is not a romantic or an emotional experience at this level.

It is a detached, impersonal, allowing experience. It is a state of being that is not personal. It is almost beyond human.

It is a different state of consciousness and yet it is a part of you. There is the human you that is having your experiences, and then there is this soul part of you that is allowing them to occur. It does not care if you keep your experiences as they are or shift them around. It does not care if you do a transformative process. It does not care if you go through life in the gutter or in a mansion. It is going to love you the same way.

When you want to shift an experience, that is what the transformative aspects of the book is about. We include this love-soul model so that you have another dimension to the work.

> MARCEY: This reminds me of the discussion around what would it be like to remove filters (removing the blue glasses or red glasses).

> MICHAEL: This is what Part Three is about, and in exploring this model we are beginning to set the stage. We work with the mind and we work with the body. What about moving beyond mind and body? What is that like?

> It seems as though there is nothing beyond mind and body—but there actually is. It is what we call spirit and it always remains undefined. The love-soul model is useful to help you be more objective, more detached and more accepting of everything that is occurring. It is simply another tool in your toolbox.

MARCEY: I like what you said, that this state and presence is always there whether we like it or not, judge it or not, judge ourself or not. It is waiting and available if we want it.

MICHAEL: Yes, all the time. All you have to do is tap into it by getting your mind out of the way. Here's another way to point to the same thing.

## Dualities and the Third State

Everything in this life is dualities, right? Black/white. Night/day. Yin/yang. You can work with these as a guide in transformation. When you want to expand your consciousness, you can bring two dualities together.

What is your conscious awareness when you combine light and dark?

A lot of times in spirituality, someone will think it has to be light, light, light all the time, but true spirituality is light and dark together. What is that third state of consciousness when you have light and dark together?

It would be the space that holds both light and dark—we could say that space is also dark but it is not dark in the same way. It is more pregnant, if you will, with the duality. You can imagine these dualities coming into existence and then popping back out of existence, back into this third state. The third state is what we will work in Part 3 which is spirit. It is also the transcendent state.

Spirit as giving rise to the multitude of dualities. The dualities arise out of the third state and eventually collapse back into the third state. Some examples are good and bad, right and wrong, black and white, night and day. The world we live in is the world of duality where everything plays with its opposite. We have this and we have that.

What happens when you get beyond your mind, beyond the conscious and unconscious aspects (which is another duality)? We have been laying this out, but spirit includes the conscious and unconscious minds together as one. Also, it includes body and mind together as one. It is the space that holds all these.

If you want to work with dualities, you must not get pigeonholed on one side or the other. You are practicing awareness, and again there is no *doing* here. We are asking you to simply notice:

▸ What is it like when you are aware of the dualities?

▸ Can you hold the dualities together in the same space? Even if they are contradictory, how do you experience the sense of paradox?

▸ What is your awareness when you have light and dark together?

▸ What happens when you bring them together in the same space?

MARCEY: In talking about dualities such as light and dark together, I'm noticing when something comes up for me, good or bad, I am also starting to notice the opposite of that state. It gives me another way to look at things when I can look at both sides. But when you have awareness of duality, there is also this third state; what do you do with that?

MICHAEL: Regarding the third state, you cannot do anything with it. *Doing* is not in that state. When a baby is gestating in your womb, you cannot make the growth happen. You can make sure you are healthy and *doing* everything to give the right environment for the fetus, but you are not making the fetus grow. It is growing through you. If you look at the metaphor of the womb, it is like this third state. You can't have the pregnancy without a container. That is what the third state is. It is the container. It is pregnant with all possibilities. It is the space that holds everything. All dualities exist in potential within that container.

Remember that this is a guide to notice different experiences within ourselves. This third state is part of the human experience that many call Spirit, Love,

Enlightenment or God. It is not something that can be *done*. It is not something that has any tangible markers to it. All you can do is tear down the concepts that keep you from experiencing it. When you begin to experience it, there is a clarity that happens. It is difficult to explain.

MARCEY: Why then be aware of this third state that holds dualities? Why is this important?

MICHAEL: It is the basis for everything that is. Nothing could be in existence without it. You could not be here without that third state. Remember, it is a mystical state so there is nothing we can define here. You have to see everything arising out of this state, having its existence and then returning back to this state. Yet paradoxically, since it is the container, it is present throughout and within our existence as well. It transcends space and time and yet is present within them! It is the same for us as well. Although the transcendent spiritual state might remain beyond one's grasp, it is always there within, patiently awaiting to be discovered. Love Transcendent and Love Inherent (beyond and within)!

There is a mystical space that each person can plug into and have their own experience of, but I cannot tell you what that will be like for you. I can only say it is there in each of us and your life changes for the positive when you begin to experience and relate to that place. If I define it, we are back into the challenge of trying to control it.

MARCEY: Is there a benefit of being in this state?

MICHAEL: Benefit? This is still the mind thinking. It has a goal, something to be gained. Even though benefits happen, this type of thinking keeps you grasping. Foster the mindset that there is nothing to be gained by this but you go there anyway.

MARCEY: What about a joyful life? Being in the flow? Developing your spiritual gifts?

MICHAEL: Absolutely. But these are byproducts that come out of it. If you go in with this mindset, if you begin to explore meditative states and mystical states with the mindset that you can get something out of it, the experience you seek will fade again into the background. Here it is helpful to understand the distinction between mind and spirit. Benefit and gain are mental strategies and they are wonderful to have as useful mental programs. It is simply that your mind and your thinking are what can keep you from your experience of spirit.

What I am doing here is greasing the wheels for the best way to enter into this state which is letting go of grasping, letting go of your expectations. Let go of the mind wanting to gain something out of going into this state. That is of the mind. That is what the mind does. It looks at the mystical space and says, "How can I control it? How can I understand it? How can I get around it?" Well, you cannot. That is the whole point. It is tricky.

Let's look more closely at one specific duality, one that will be most useful in understanding your place in the world.

## Uniqueness and Oneness

One of the dualities, one of the primary ones in our work, is uniqueness and oneness. The duality of being completely unique in your individuality and completely like everyone else, connected and the same as everyone.

What is it like when those two can coexist? What is your experience when you can be completely unique/different and completely the same as others - at the same time?

It is important to get to your uniqueness. This is part of the reason for the work around identity—who you are. The key is to realize there is only one of you on the planet and there is no roadmap for being that you. You are blazing that trail. That is what uniqueness is about. You are unique. When you are unique, how could you possibly look outside yourself for any validation?

Paradoxically, when you are unique, this is also what plugs you into sameness, into oneness. When you get to your center and realize, "I am totally unique. I am lovable, as I am", then you are also able to plug into the greater unity and focus on what you are being called to share with the world.

This is opening the door to section three about living our purpose. That is why the book is structured the way it is. We first talked about individuality, who are you and getting to your true self. It gets to be about self.

When you are that unique self and knowing yourself as good, whole and complete, then you no longer need outside validation. Then it becomes about how you express that unique self out into the world. Then the work is going to change direction and go back outward. Paradoxically, it's about changing our attention back to the external world and being able to be present to others.

## ⚡ KEY CONCEPT

*Once you understand and appreciate your uniqueness, you can plug back into the greater world, the greater unity with the gifts that are unique to you, gifts to be shared with the world.*

## Beyond Your Mind-Body

We are going deeper beyond body and mind where you no longer need or focus on self. As you want to move forward into purpose, you need to get over self.

That does not mean that the inner work on self is done. You are going to have to go back and visit self much of the time, but you do not have to do it 24/7. If you get triggered, or if you want to work with a pattern, it will be about self. Then when you are going out into the world and living your purpose, it is no longer about you. It is going to be about the other people, about us - the we vs. me.

At a certain point we become free of the need for any attention from other people.

Imagine that you no longer needed anyone's attention or any validation in any way because you were so adequately self-validated that you felt complete and whole. Your tank was full from the inside out. With this experience you are able to give others your undivided attention. You might say, "Okay, great. Got that. Now how do I take that out into the world? How can I go live that out into the world in a way that it does not have to be about me anymore?"

That is how we move toward spirit. The use of spirit in this context is saying it is the larger field of us together as a whole species, as the whole planet basically. As an individual, you have a part to play and you plug into a greater unity, to a totality. You can only do that when you get to your true self, to your true authentic essence.

Do the work to deconstruct and transform your patterns until you know you are okay just the way you are. This helps you be in touch with what your life is about or what is important to you. Then how do you bring that out into the world? How do you live that out into the world?

Let's take this notion of self a bit further. Let's discuss, "Letting go of the need to self-define and discover your true identity."

What happens when you are comfortable enough with yourself that you no longer need a self-definition? You could say, "Okay, my true identity is the mystery unfolding as the incarnation called (insert your name)." The language gets a little funny at this stage because everything in our language is self-oriented (I am this, I am that).

However, this is the stage when it does not have to be about self anymore. It involves self because you have to know yourself, what you are interested in and what your passions are. Yet in order to move into the transcendent state, the guiding principle is: let us get over self now.

Can you consider living as the unfolding mystery of who you are, such that you defy definition?

The metaphor I use for this is a flower continually in bloom for all eternity.

You are always blooming from this place of spirit in the container of love. You are always blooming and it will keep informing and guiding you as well. Self is not a static thing. You learn, grow, change and evolve. It is an ongoing process throughout your entire life.

MARCEY: When I think of some of the issues I'm working through, there is part of me that says, "Okay, if I resolve that, then what?" My body issues, my self-judgment issues, etc. Then who will I be after that?

MICHAEL: In fact, you are not these issues. That is part of the problem. You may have been identified with the issues and they are not who you are. If we can get to a place where our identity does not have to be defined, then to me that is the best identity to have.

I am going to live out my separate self, my unique self, but in my mind I do not have to have the "I" defined. I do not have to say, "Oh, I am a person who likes pomegranates." That is my personal preference. I love pomegranates. But I do not have to go through the process of defining myself by that. Or judging those who do not like pomegranates!

In a silly way this is something that divides us— my preferences and needs and judgment of others, or myself over you, which is in essence judging myself. It is designed to keep us separate.

That is the illusion when we get to this stage, and this is a beautiful transition for moving into Part Three.

It is this transition where we no longer need the illusion of separateness. I have got enough of my uniqueness in place that I do not need to constantly keep "self-ing". It can now be about "us", about this connected greater reality that everyone has access to if we go deep enough.

> ### o⃗ KEY CONCEPT
>
> *What divides us is our preferences, needs and judgement of others or myself over you, which in essence is judging ourselves. This is designed to keep us separate and that is an illusion.*

It lies beyond and yet it is always present; it is the space that is allowing our human experience.

How do we live that? Does it mean without needing? Without wanting?

We will still have needs and wants. Those don't go away. But the key is to be in touch with them, to work with those needs and wants. Then to be able to dis-identify from them so that one can go into that greater reality as well.

> MARCEY: Yeah, that is a good motivation to overcome obstacles - they are distracting. Now I see how you could show up to a session with somebody and see their whole self.

> MICHAEL: When you know the essence in yourself, you see it in other people too. That is the starting point when I offer a session, I am in that place. Then I can see the other person against the backdrop of spirit. How is this person showing up? How are they expressing self? What are they believing in? Can I get them to see what is great about them apart from how their filters might be operating?

> MARCEY: Being in this space does not necessary mean that you have no boundaries. Being your full self may mean that you have boundaries and do not let people walk all over you.

> MICHAEL: Of course. In the beginning of the journey, when we first get to the mountaintop, we might think we need to get rid boundaries. However, boundaries are a crucial part of the second stage, coming back to the village. You come back to the village as a changed person because of your mountaintop experience, but you need to have a way for healthy interaction with the world. Even though you are getting beyond yourself, you need to maintain your boundaries.

While Part Two was mostly about the body and about overcoming obstacles, in this last chapter we went beyond that theme. This was done as a primer for what is to come in the next part of the book. However, before moving on we will do our usual review.

## Let's recap the key concepts from Part Two:

- ▸▸ Without our bodies we would not have experiences. Through the practice of noticing how our bodies respond to the external world, we create a new level of understanding ourselves.

- ▸▸ When you can begin to listen to the intelligence of your body, it will lead you to people, places and events that are correct for you.

- ▸▸ VAKOG refers to the five senses that we use to collect information that then runs through the programs in our brain to create our reality.

- ▸▸ An "access" or "access point" is means of getting to the key driver for an experience—what actually marks and creates an experience in your brain.

- ▸▸ While outer obstacles exist, they have an inner experience that is self-created. Deconstructing this can bring a powerful shift in your consciousness and give you the opportunity to have a more positive experience.

- ▸▸ You can have an impact on obstacles that show up in your life if you begin to notice and recognize patterns of obstacles and any memories relevant to them.

- ▸▸ The Law of Attraction does not work if there are unconscious beliefs counter to what you want to attract.

- ▸▸ Transforming your experiences requires seeing the underlying structure within the experience.

- ▸▸ It is not what you are aware of that is the problem; it is what you are not aware of. Tenacious obstacles almost always have an unconscious attachment that you are not aware of.

- ▸▸ Being triggered is not bad or wrong, but it may take us out of our place of peace, joy and calm. The practice is getting back to this more enjoyable state rather than trying to avoid triggers altogether.

- ▸▸ It is important to replace unwanted behaviors with something wanted, else once the unwanted behavior is not there, the mind can be left to spin.

- There are filtering systems in your brain that make things seem different than they actually are because they are reinterpreting what is happening through filters created from the past.

- Time traveling is a way to bring your current wisdom and self to your past as a way to inform or reassure your younger self. This process can be transformational.

- In Jungian psychology archetypes represent universal patterns and images that are part of the collective unconscious. Jung believed that we inherit these archetypes much in the way we inherit instinctive patterns of behavior. Begin to see the themes that come about in your life.

- Evolutionary influences are typically unconscious, but we can learn to be aware of them and the influence they may have in our lives.

- The love-soul model is not romantic or emotional love; it is a state of being.

- Once you understand and appreciate your uniqueness, you can plug back into the greater world, the greater unity with the gifts that are unique to you, that are to be shared with the world.

- What divides us is our preferences, needs, and judgment of others, or of ourself over others which in essence is judging ourselves. This is designed to keep us separate and that is an illusion.

By now we have journeyed quite a way into your interior life. We've explored the workings of your mind, both in its conscious aspects and in the unconscious aspects (as they relate to the body and the brain). We covered a number of tools for raising awareness and transforming limiting patterns. We are now ready to go deeply into the spiritual aspect of your journey—to the mountaintop and back. As we have said, this is about getting beyond yourself yet always inclusive of it. We are ready to jump into Part Three, the world of Spirit, and how this relates to living your purpose in the world.

Part Three:
# LIVING PURPOSE

▲ ▲ ▲

# CHAPTER 15

# The Third Guiding Question: The Mystical Nature of Your Purpose

## Third Guiding Question–What are you really here to do?

The unfolding of this question brings you to your purpose. But this question contains a challenge to discover more about what your true purpose really is. The question is: "What are you really here to do?" I mean really.

When we ask "What are you really here to do?" it does not have to always be a grandiose mission. It can be that you are here to be kind to the people you encounter throughout your day or you are here to raise your family in the best possible way. Maybe you are here to work with the elderly. Maybe it's working with better ecology in our environment. Whatever it is, it touches those around you in a wonderful way. For me I am here to work with people to wake up as much as possible to the benefit of humanity in my own unique way. My purpose was a big factor in creating this book.

But purpose goes far beyond these bigger themes. It is more about how you bring it into your everyday reality. Sometimes people get a little too hung up on purpose, as if they are going to have some flash and then know exactly what they are here to do. While this can happen, it doesn't always work that way. I see it as an unfolding. The doing is not like a goal type of doing. It involves a passive listening; listening for the intuitive guidance within you. Now when we ask what are you *really* here to do, we could also ask it as: what is spirit asking of you? What is this mystical state asking you to do? How are you being called and are you willing to fully answer that call?

It may not always be something you want to do. Maybe your individuality does not always want to be "on" all the time, or maybe sometimes you do not feel like helping others. This is okay and part of the experience. Those feelings are part of the mix. If you are in touch with your center and your spirit, then this begins to create an energetic field that is greater than your feelings or thoughts. You find it through your individuality, but it does not come from it. It is something greater than self but always passing through self from within.

Does your purpose unfold or evolve over time?

Yes. We are each doing our best from our current state of consciousness. But your consciousness evolves over time and your purpose might as well. It requires a constant listening for your inner guidance. Maybe your intention is too grandiose: "I have to have the biggest impact on the biggest amount of people or else I am not living my purpose." This can be faulty thinking. Or maybe you are not thinking big enough. "I do not think I can make a difference."

You might start something by going in a certain direction and it fulfills you for a while. But after some time, it could no longer fulfill you and you may desire change. Maybe a course correction is needed or a new direction altogether, like a high-powered CEO who makes a career change to starting a restaurant because they realize their love of cooking. Or maybe your direction is correct but something deeper is happening with you. You might have to adjust what you are doing or adjust your belief system. It depends on the person and the context. There is no hard and fast rule.

Many people are already living their purpose without realizing it. Sometimes it is what you do naturally when you are not thinking about it or aware of it. You have probably helped or touched more people than you realize by being authentically yourself. It could even be through your career. For example, one's purpose may be to help create more ease for people through organizational gifts or to help facilitate more compassionate and clear meetings. How do you support your direct reports or coworkers to fulfill their job function better? It is a shift in orientation, a new way of seeing the world.

As you continue to explore deeper into the mystical state, one effect is positive change. It changes your thoughts, it changes your feelings, it changes your body, and it changes the energy you are working with. Once you are operating from a place of spiritual purpose, you engage a mysterious "something more" factor. Internally or personally, not much may seem to be happening, but more and more you become a conduit for powerful experiences in others.

What others might see as magic, serendipitous, or even miraculous begins to seem more normal and seems to occur more frequently.

It can be quite a relief because you do not have to do it all yourself. You are part of something greater and you belong. You only need to show up. You only need to play your part. You live out your purpose when you engage back into society as your authentic self.

Earlier in the book we discussed the mountaintop experience and returning to the village. It could be one's spiritual purpose to sit on the mountaintop and never return to the village. Then they are called to play the part of the hermit. There are hermits and recluses in the world. If someone is authentically called to that, it can be a very powerful purpose helping in ways beyond what we might understand. But that is also a very difficult life and only very few are truly called in this way.

Most of us are called to live in the world, back in the village where our purpose unfolds in the world. But this is where one might get tripped up... wanting changes in the world around them, but not so much in themselves. We want the joy in the external world we are living in, in our environments, in our activities and in our relationships. But as we have learned, that can only come from inside. Once you are operating from your center, it does affect those around you. It affects others because you become a conduit for spirit to enter into your current reality. You create heaven on earth. You bring the spiritual state into the earthly state. You ground the spiritual in the physical world through your humanity. This is everyone's true purpose, and how each of us does this is entirely unique.

Could someone's purpose involve their own struggle or suffering, things that are not "light and love"?

I think it is how someone does that. In your purpose if you are really going to wake up, you must be willing to face your inner pain. There are most likely going to be painful, struggling and suffering moments in everyone's life. How do you go through those times? Do you do it as a little child, kicking and screaming? Or as a mature adult? Do you blame other people, or do you take an honest look in the mirror about what is really going on within you? Every human being goes through painful moments in life. Living in spirit helps you get through life's difficult moments with grace and equanimity.

Suffering can be a tricky word. Depending on how you go through a particular experience, you can suffer through it or you can endure it. Some different questions come to mind. Does someone need to suffer? What is suffering? Doesn't each of us suffer in our own way? How do you define suffering?

One person might have physical pain and another person might have mental anguish. Yet they are both suffering in some way. In certain cases, you just have to go through it, endure it. Some people go through needless suffering because they are caught in unresolved pain from their past. This is when you want to apply our transformational tools from Parts One and Two. However, once you live from your spiritual center, you might still suffer at times, but usually gracefully and rarely needlessly.

Love or spirit is always waiting patiently for you, and it seems that your purpose is being a channel for spirit or love regardless of the specifics of how you live that out.

Love is within you. It is your true nature. Go within to your center, connect with your loving nature, know you are unique, precious, and one of a kind. Then ask, "How does my uniqueness fit in and belong in the world?"

When you are unique, how do you plug into the world? What are you here to do as your unique self? Not as your conditioned self, but as the true you?

This whole journey of individuality from the first two parts of the book is what you need to undertake before you can more authentically live out your purpose. If you do not know who and what you are, and you are trying to live your purpose, it is not going to be your real purpose.

## 🔑 KEY CONCEPT

*Once you know who you are, then you begin to know what you are really here to do.*

Once you know who you are, then you begin to know what you are really here to do.

Usually, people want the "doing" before the "being." But this is the being before the doing. Once you know your being, your purpose unfolds out of that—you being authentically you. Then do what you would naturally do and you will be living out your purpose.

MARCEY: Around five years ago I talked to somebody about purpose and the industry I am in which is banking and lending credit. How could my work in a bank (with its intentions of making money with interest and fees) be an extension of me living out my purpose? The answer I got was that banks need people who are especially living their life purpose. These people are needed to bring organization to new projects, to set up and teach programs, to give opportunities by funding small businesses, and to make difficult choices such as closing out credit when someone may get overextended. It is up to these people as to how they are going to use credit. After understanding that, I started looking for opportunities to mentor other people at work and find ways to bring who I am—individually, spiritually, mentally, physically—into this infrastructure that is not typically seen as kind or loving.

MICHAEL: Thank you for sharing that. It's a great example of living one's purpose in the world around them.

An important aspect of this book is getting to this part and saying, "Now I am going to let spirit unfold *and* I want to live my purpose in the world." Does this mean surrendering by doing nothing or jumping back into action? It is very much both in a cosmic dance. It is living out the duality of the passive and the active, of the yin and yang aspects of life.

As you proceed, consider the unification of spirit and purpose. They go hand in hand. When you are living out your spiritual purpose, your attention needs to go back to the outside world and how you show up. Much of this book has been about the internal world and eventually getting to the mystical state of "non-doing." But here the focus is external by bringing your attention back out into the world and focusing on your actions in the world. As you continue to explore your mystical center within you, your purpose unfolds outside of you. It must take place in your

## 🔑 KEY CONCEPT

*As you continue to explore your mystical center, your purpose unfolds outside of you.*

relationships, in your actions, and in how you are present in the world around you.

What do you do with that? How is this beneficial?

There is something that each of us is here to express out into the world. Consider your individuality, your uniqueness, and what you are deeply passionate about. These are giving you clues about your true purpose. While purpose involves getting beyond self, it is through your authentic self that you find it.

## Your Place in The Greater Unity

There is a greater unity that we are all a part of. As human beings most of us cannot understand the entire picture of this greater unity with our current state of consciousness. It remains greater than any individual can get their head around. You could imagine some greater collective consciousness, but does anyone truly know the whole picture? Actually, you do not need to. You are on a need-to-know basis. You are only here to tend to the portion that you tend to—which is your perspective on reality. Each person has to do that authentically, being true to oneself.

In finding your part in the greater unity, your individuality is the access point. It is through your individuality that you begin to understand what you are really here to do. Remember, once you know who you are, then you begin to know what you are really here to do.

# CHAPTER 16

▲ ▲ ▲

# Exploring Your Purpose

## Clues to Finding Your Purpose

Within finding your purpose lies another paradox and challenge. While living true to your individuality in the world, you are also accessing this inner "something more", this mystical state. You access this by getting beyond being self-focused or self-absorbed. However, in living out your purpose, you need to also honor your uniqueness, the part of you that is authentically self. This means inwardly you need to practice no-self while outwardly you need to be authentically yourself.

When you put your focus back out into the world, you need to express your individuality. As you do that, there are things specific to your individuality, to who you are, that tend to grab your attention. Those are the areas of interest you want to pay attention to. What really grabs you? What really lights you up?

Out of all the world has to offer, what gets you feeling most alive?

For example, we are creating this book because we are passionate about the field of spiritual development and transformation; we are not writing a romance novel. Now there is absolutely nothing wrong with romance novels, but they're not my thing. They might be someone else's purpose. It is about the things that really grab your attention. In that grain if you begin to look at your passions, the things that you are truly deeply passionate about, the things that are grabbing your attention in life, you are probably uniquely endowed to have some gift in that direction. You can begin to explore your listening to and trusting of the mystery within that knows you have a part to play when you are true to your authentic self.

What are you here to look at? To give your attention to? What are your gifts? How are you best of service? How do you fit into this thing called life? Each of us is like a puzzle piece and we all fit together somehow. But the overall picture is a mystery. Your piece of the puzzle is your purpose... the unfolding of that. You gain more clarity as you take a step in that direction. Again the answers might take time to unfold.

### Exercise

Consider your hobbies, passions and interests. What are you most excited about? Begin to brainstorm.

This is an exercise in imagination—do not let your critical mind limit yourself.

Begin to let your imagination play without censorship. What are different ways that you could be living out your passions? Simply imagine!

What does it feel like to let these imaginations play?

Notice the experience when you let yourself imagine in this way.

These are clues to your purpose.

## Your Medium of Expression

As you explore your purpose, it is important to also ask "How do I get out into the world and share these gifts?" When you know who you are and what you have to offer, then you must ask: How? How are you going to do that? What medium are you using?

For instance, I meet with clients one on one and do workshops and retreats. I also wrote this book. This is the medium of how I am sharing my gifts with the world. This is what you also need to look at. What is the medium of your expression? If you are an artist, are you working with paint, clay or something else? What is the medium for your expression out into the world? If you are a programmer, what code are you using? As a team leader, what are you doing to keep your people on track? How do you communicate with those around you? Your voice (tone, frequency, rate, pitch, etc.) and your movement are also mediums for your expression.

When you explore your expression, it supports you in living your purpose. One might feel like a freak, falsely believing they do not fit into the world, but that is a limiting identity. The more you honor your uniqueness and how you express that, the more you actually DO fit in. Other people will respond to your uniqueness. Other people will have issues with you when you have those same issues with yourself. When you clear those issues within yourself, then the world stops having those issues with you. Then the world sees and treats you differently.

Your expression or your frequency—it is like putting out a beacon. When it is clear, people respond to you differently. If you are still operating from a conditioned place, your expression is not going to be clear. It may resonate with some people, but maybe not as universally and maybe not with the people you're supposed to reach. The way comes through being YOU as you operate as your true self!

> MARCEY: One of my husband's gifts is connecting with people. He shows up as a tall strong garbageman in a loud dirty truck. From the outside he seems like a tough heavy-equipment operator. But he has amazing relationships with customers, the community he serves and his coworkers. One could think that, in his industry, to have a gift of connection seems an unlikely medium for a garbageman.

> MICHAEL: This is a great example of a medium. He is bringing his gifts to his customers and the people he touches. It is not industry dependent. It does not matter where or in what field of life you are in; it matters more about how you show up and if you are being yourself. In doing that you will tend to naturally express your gifts without having to think about it.

Now having explored your unfolding purpose, let's take a deeper dive into the spiritual dimension—what spirit means, and how to keep working with it in service of living your purpose.

# CHAPTER 17

▲ ▲ ▲

# The Meaning of Spirit and "Something More"

When we use the word spirit or spiritual, we have to steer clear of what it means. It presents a problem because it can have so many different meanings.

As human beings we need and want meaning. We do. We are each creating our own meaning of everything. Furthermore, the meanings we make are deeply personal. Humans are meaning-making machines; this is what our minds do. It is normal and natural. Meaning is very important to each of us and again very personal. Yet something only has meaning if we create the meaning.

Remember the three distinctions in your cognitive awareness? Let's review them:

- First, are the raw experiences put together by sensory-based information, the Vs, As, and Ks.

- Then a layer up from that, we make meaning of these raw experiences.

- Then a layer up from meaning is language, where we talk about the meaning in our attempt to communicate and be understood.

When an experience is deep and spiritual, often the translation to language becomes difficult. There are not a lot of words because the language to describe it becomes limited. The meaning might seem like the "something more" factor. Something is happening. You may not fully understand it, but you can sense into it. Any meaning that occurs is deeply personal and created in your mind. However, because of the transcendent nature of spirit, we could say, that at the level of spirit there is no meaning.

A state of no meaning is not a comfortable state for people. It goes right up against wanting meaning. Many of us say, "I want life to mean something. I want it to be important." The spiritual dimension is the most important part of our life, but it must remain forever free of any interpretation. Consider that meaning is a translation of "something more" into your personal life, into how your individuality perceives the mystical state and reality. But what are we talking about in getting beyond meaning?

## Beyond Meaning and into Presence

Meaning throughout history has typically been dealt with by religions, but they also do a great job of helping us get beyond meaning. The Buddhists do a particularly good job at tearing away the constructs of the mind. "No meaning, no mind" is the Buddhist approach. The Heart Sutra in Buddhism tears away everything; no senses, no mind, no meaning, no consciousness, no nothing. In the Vedic tradition they say neti-neti. Not this, not that. In mystical Christianity there is the practice of the Apophatic approach, a prayer with no content. These traditions are pointing to a mystical unitive state that lies within and beyond. To go there means getting beyond the mind and its need for meaning.

In order to explore this further, we are going to do as much as we can to tear down concepts, tear down everything that keeps you from sensing into and from your own spiritual heart. Paradox is very useful at this point because it disrupts the mind, especially if you are in your mind trying to figure out spirit. Again it is like the snake trying to swallow a buffalo. It is too big for the mind to get around. Paradox is when you disrupt the mental process or when something seems to not make sense. When the mind is disrupted, it often results in confusion and yet this can be very useful!

In certain sects of Buddhism, they use the koan, an unsolvable riddle. Examples of these can be found in many texts. They are often complex and used to illustrate different lessons in various ways. Here are some of the more famous very short ones:

▹ Two hands clap and there is a sound. What is the sound of one hand clapping?

▹ Two monks are arguing about a flag. One says, "The flag is moving." The other, "The wind is moving." A third walks by and says, "Not the wind, not the flag; the mind is moving."

▸ What was your original face before your mother and father were born?

Contemplating these exercises can almost be disturbing in how they disrupt the mind. Yet this is exactly what to do in order to begin to experience spirit. It does not have to be constant. You can go back to everyday life and back to thinking about things. But in a retreat moment, in a mountaintop moment, you want to get to a point of tearing down thinking and analyzing.

> MARCEY: In thinking about paradox and duality, oppos-
> ing things that seem at odds in our life could both be true.
> If we can live in that pregnant place of the third state of
> letting go of judging good or bad, right or wrong, bet-
> ter—best—worst, and of realizing that there are infinite
> possibilities; all could be true at the same time.

> MICHAEL: Yes! This is the place of the unknown, and
> humans generally have a fear of the unknown. This is
> why people tend to resist. Unless an experience is known
> or defined, there is a natural tendency in human beings
> to resist it.

In referring to the third state, the "something more" factor or spirit, I prefer to use the word mystery or mystical. I find it is easier to relate to, but it is different for everyone. Source and love are also nice terms. Many people call it God. In some of the Eastern traditions they call it voidness or emptiness. We want to make sure when someone uses the terms voidness, emptiness, nothing, no-mind, or no-self, that we are not talking about a complete absence. This is nihilism and it is not the correct path. Nihilism is where you feel there is nothing, only a blank dead space. That is different from the true experience of spirit. You might not be able to experience it directly, but spirit is pregnant with all possibilities. It might seem empty like air, but it is not. We are making a distinction between nihilistically empty and empty in a spiritual sense which is full, but appears empty to our perception. So how do you begin to access this state?

Our access point as human beings is to begin to get still and silent.

Silence,

Stillness,

Calming,

Stopping,

Just for a moment.

Stop.

It could be only for a moment. Maybe for a moment you are not thinking of anything or feeling anything in your body. Or not emoting. Maybe you are not having any experience (which is its own experience).

What would your experience be if for a moment you are sitting still, calm and silent—not thinking, not feeling and not sensing anything?

I knew one guy from the monastery who said, "Even no experience is an experience." For a moment we might experience "no experience" which is itself a unique kind of experience. Yes, it's a paradox. It is an experience in itself, but it is the experience of not having an immediate experience. What is that? Imagine a container and the contents within the container. It is noticing the container without any content in it. Now let go of even the concept of the container.

These are more koans. They are going to point you to something that can't be spoken or discussed. Stop trying to figure it out and simply "be" for a moment. If you are confused, let your confusion be.... it's part of the process.

What's behind your thinking? Again, when nothing is happening, it is still a particular kind of experience.

You still exist, right? Can you notice the backdrop of that? You are still alive. Your heart is still beating. You are still here, but you are having an experience of not experiencing anything directly for a moment...a clear state.

Once you begin to have a few experiences of stillness, then it becomes a resting place. It becomes a place you can always go to. It not only creates the magic and creates that "something more" factor, but it also gives you a home within. It gives you a safe space to come into where you can always rest. It gives you the opportunity to take a break from everything going on in the outside world and recharge your batteries. It can feel very rejuvenating to simply rest at peace in this place!

As you begin to live your spiritual purpose out into the world, you must still visit the mystical space. It is important to go back as much as possible in order to recharge. As an embodiment of spirit in the world, you need to come back to your spiritual home within. Then you can go back out and do your work in the world again.

Imagine this process of living outwardly, but always from your internal spiritual center. When you live in the world from your center, it has an effect. You cannot predict what that effect is going to be because spirit is beyond your intentions. But somehow the world responds differently when you come from spirit.

Here is the challenge.... I can only point to this place in you now. When you sit still, when you let everything calm down; maybe it is going to take a day, maybe it is going to take a month, maybe it is going to take a year, maybe it is going to take a minute. But when you sit still and the mind calms down, suddenly it is like the clear surface of a lake. The water gets still and there are no ripples anymore. You are not emoting or feeling anything about anything, yet there is a deep and abiding peace. Maybe you are more in touch with your body at this point. Maybe you are simply a body breathing. Maybe you are not in a particular experience in the body. Yet you are still alive!

## Exercise

Sit still, keep your spine straight and notice the simple experience of your body breathing.

Do not try to alter your breath in any way—notice it as it is.

At some point you might notice a deeper breath occurring naturally; allow it to happen. Allow your breath to deepen naturally if this occurs.

If your mind starts to wander, this is okay. Simply bring your mind back to the experience of breathing.

This is a simple breathing meditation.

When I meditate, I tend to notice more of my body level experience. When I do this, I note the experience and let it be there without doing anything with it. Then I allow it to pass, let it go, and come back to breathing and stillness. Noticing and letting it pass... noticing, letting it pass...noticing, letting it pass. Eventually this calms down as well.

Eventually you come to presence.

> MARCEY: This is the something else. This is the something more. This is presence. We can focus on the breath, but what about the time in between breaths?

> MICHAEL: Beautiful! This is the space between. We could say, in music it is the space between the notes that really makes the music. You cannot have sound without the silence. You cannot have movement without stillness. You cannot have any event or experience without the empty space to contain it.

The mystical state is always available. You come into life and you get to live your life, but your life is coming from this state. The more you rest in this state, the more it guides you from within. It becomes your inner guide.

### ⚷ KEY CONCEPT

*When you are able to sit in the still, empty space, that is your mountaintop. It has its own intelligence. This state becomes your inner guide.*

That stillness or emptiness, while it is no experience in itself, affects your body, affects your mind, affects your emotions, and affects how you relate to people and how they relate to you. It guides you from within you and is the key to your presence.

We usually sense something in presence. Being around others living from this state opens you up and invites you to be present as well. The name on my website is "Loving Presence Embodiment" (www.loveguides.us) because that is what each of us is: loving presence embodied. It is the Loving Presence within you that others respond to.

But how do you know if you are present?

The etymology of present is to be pre-sent. This is also a little koan. It's almost as though something is divinely ordered. In a funny sort of way, you can see it as though you were called, you were sent, you were pre-sent. You are showing up to be here at this time in the right place right now. You are present.

It can only happen in the here and now. Consider the intersection of time and space. This particular moment...where you are in space at this particular time. Are you allowing yourself to show up at that precise intersection? Not in your mind thinking about yesterday or tomorrow. Not sitting here in this space thinking about being somewhere else. You are here in this moment.

But who is the one present?

Remember at the beginning of Part One we discussed the difference between your individual and your spiritual identity. Is presence you in your individuality or is it something greater?

Consider that the real key to presence is allowing something greater to come through your individuality.

Sometimes that something greater is coming through you and you are not aware of it. You might not know that you are having an effect on other people. Sometimes when you are preoccupied and going about your life, there is still a positive impact. If you are not always aware and intentional, this is okay. Do the best you can and be kind and gentle as you work with your presence. Mostly, if you do your inner work and be clear within yourself, it will affect other people in a positive way.

 **KEY CONCEPT**

*The key to presence is allowing something greater to come through your individuality.*

> MARCEY: This is not on the mountaintop; this is in the village, right?

> MICHAEL: Yes, when you are out in the world and present, that is the return to the village. But the presence comes from your experience of being on the mountaintop. You have got to have the mountaintop reference point.

You must first know that experience, and then practice how you express that out in the world.

If someone only sits in silence and stillness, this can be a powerful purpose. This is what we call being on the mountaintop. But unless you are called to be a hermit, you still need to engage and live in the world around you. That is the return to the village. The key to presence is to let the mountaintop shine through you while you are interacting in the outside world. What happens when you bring the mountaintop down into the village?

MARCEY: I have noticed quite a shift with this spirit work. I have lived most of my life from my neck up with my mind constantly processing like a computer. Now I have spent more time connecting my mind with my body. Once I notice my mind, and how that machine is working, and how my body is feeling, then I pause and notice my center. By letting go of control and observing this body, mind, spirit connection, I can then show up in a space of curiosity about what I need to do for my day from this place of center. This for me is living in my purpose. I have noticed many things showing up that align with my passions and interests.

MICHAEL: As we have discussed, we cannot say much about spirit, yet we can point to it. What is also important is the integration. This is what some people miss. Spirit is not separate. We talk about it as a separate experience, but the return to the village is an integration where mind, body and spirit come together. Spirit remains in charge. We give the reins over to spirit, but we still have to live that through our bodies and minds.

MARCEY: What is transformational about this work is that you do not only honor and connect with spirit on a particular day of the week, or in the quietness of your home, or as you are going to sleep; but that you are also integrating spirit into your life: at work, at home, with everyone you interact with—friends and strangers. This feels like living through spirit throughout your daily life.

## The Yearning of the Heart

In Sufi literature and in Christian mysticism, there is a lot of writing on the desire of the heart. The yearning of the heart is different from a grasping or a craving that Buddhism talks about. Sometimes in the west, desire gets a bad rap, but desire is another way to get into the mystical state. When you feel desire as its own experience without trying to fill it up, this is the desire of the heart.

If you can sit in the space of the yearning of your heart, your heart wants to know love. It wants to know your completeness and it wants to know God. You can call those by different names, but the experience itself feels as if possibly something is missing—where we are trying to find ourselves or yearn for the ultimate life, the ultimate experience. What many people tend to miss is sometimes the experience of the yearning itself is the mystical state.

We discussed this in Part Two, but it bears repeating. If we can be in the yearning, be in the desire without trying to fill it up, it opens up into its own experience as a mystical state. Sometimes feeling empty in our heart can be a portal to a breakthrough. It can be a portal that leads us to something deeper, leads us to our spirit, leads us to our mystical state.

> ### 🔑 KEY CONCEPT
>
> *If we can be in the yearning and in the desire for something without trying to fill it up, it opens up its own experience as a mystical state.*

The key is to not try to fill it (or fulfill it) with anything—to stay in the emptiness, to stay in the spaciousness.

My good friend, Father Daniel, said, "God is close when you feel the desire for God as much as when you feel the fulfillment of God." Desire is the other side of the coin of the fulfillment of the desire. We think we feel complete when we feel the fulfillment of that desire, but we can also feel as complete in the yearning for the fulfillment. They go hand in hand and they are both part of the mystical state.

The nice part about this way is that by going into the heart, much of the time we bypass the analytical function of the mind which tries to figure things out. What we have to develop is the capacity to sit in the yearning, to feel the desire itself as its own experience.

> MARCEY: Is this something that we would want to practice as an openness throughout the day?

> MICHAEL: Of course, practice as much as possible. In my own experience I do not feel the yearning all the time—it arises in moments. I would say this is not an everyday experience because to get to that level of depth is not common. We are busy with our lives, and it is not common to always be in touch at that level where we are feeling this state.

> The key is that if we feel desire for something, can we work with that? Try to take it to this level rather than getting in the distraction or the feeding of the desire. You cannot architect this because the desire of the heart is not something you have control over. It arises when it arises; you are present with it when it is present. Remember, as you work with the spirit and the mystical state, you realize you are not in control of that part of the process. You are simply listening with your heart for something beyond you.

> MARCEY: Is this more of a mountaintop feeling?

> MICHAEL: Yes, that is complete mountaintop. If you sit with the yearning of your heart, it is the mountaintop— they are one in the same. However, in this approach it is through feeling. You feel as though something is missing and you are aching for something, aching for love. If you go into it and you sit with it and allow it, you will

find a place where nothing is missing. There is fullness and completeness in that space that feels initially like something is missing. But the only way to do it is to go through it whenever it arises.

It is not something one can dig around and pull up because it is as if the spirit implants this desire at the center of each us. It is an implanted desire to know oneness, love or God, and it keeps us questing. This is beyond choice at this stage. All we can do is begin to explore and trust that there is a process going on that we are part of it; and it is very intimately involving us, but we are not in charge of it.

This leads us to trusting spirit within—trusting that there is something going on in our spiritual life even though we are not architecting it ourselves.

# CHAPTER 18

▲ ▲ ▲ ▲

# Trusting Spirit Within

## Learning/Beginner's Mind

*"In the beginner's mind there are many possibilities,*
*but in the expert's there are few."*
~Shunryu Suzuki, Zen Mind, Beginner's Mind

In Zen Buddhism they talk about "beginner's mind." This means that when you start something, you have a fresh mind regarding what you are learning. You tend to remain more engaged as if approaching it for the first time. The concept of beginner's mind is that you can stay in this first time mindset even if you are an expert in your field. Imagine you are always just beginning your journey even if you are well into it. It is always possible to say, "Okay, I am starting today. This is my first day."

Along with the continual learning that can happen in life, the beginner's mindset helps you get beyond the ego. It helps you get beyond the need to identify as a wise person and to have the answers. If you are constantly a student of life and a student of spirit, your learning is going to continue. Once you think you know it all, you hit a trap of falling back into an over-inflated sense of self. However, if you stay in a beginner's mindset, stay in learning as an orientation, it works as an ego check. It keeps you in a healthy mode on your spiritual journey.

Learning is a constant in life and everyone learns differently. Some people do better with body learning, some with repetition, some with visual cues, others with auditory methods. It depends how you are oriented and how you best learn. The key is to explore how you learn best and to take the ego out of the process. Beyond how you learn, consider that when you learn about spirit, there is nothing to figure out. There are only things being revealed in using awareness and noticing more—what we have been suggesting throughout this book. This means practicing, learning, becoming more awake and more aware on your own journey and as your own guide.

As you approach spiritual practice, it can be difficult to enter into this undefined territory. This is when the concept of beginner's mind can be very useful. Even if you have a very advanced spiritual awareness, it is best to approach it as if you are just starting.

## Surrender/Giving Up Control

When we talk about surrendering, let's make a distinction. In Part Two we talked about the transformative parts of inner experiences, the ones in which you have a choice to change. However, there is another class of experiences for human beings that are beyond our control. It is for these types of experiences that we can benefit by working with surrender.

Surrender is not giving up. In fact, it is the opposite. You are fully engaged while you are allowing experience to arise in your awareness without resisting. You are not surrendering to others or to situations outside of yourself. It is a surrender to stop fighting against what needs to be seen internally. If there is a pattern to be transformed, you need to surrender in your awareness so that you can more accurately notice what is happening. It is a process of surrendering to what is arising at deeper and deeper levels of your interior life.

Surrender is mostly about giving up control of the inner world. The word control comes from the etymology counter + roll. If we are rolling forward with something, control is counter to that rolling. While control is useful when it comes to one's behavior, it can operate as a counter force to making spiritual progress.

There is an important dimension to surrender in regards certain experiences which are beyond our control. There are times in life where people have painful experiences that cannot be changed. There are good and innocent people who experience very difficult situations and circumstances. Sometimes painful things happen. This is when surrender becomes a useful approach.

We want to make sure we are not falling into victimhood which we explored in earlier parts of the book, but sometimes things happen to us, sometimes very painful things. For instance, innocent people who are affected by wars. They might have lost loved ones in a bomb attack. There are people who have been impacted by natural disasters and lose their homes. They had no control over such events as hurricanes, earthquakes, tsunamis or fires. These are something beyond anyone's individual power.

## Cause and Effect in Relation to Control

> MARCEY: When we talk about the mystical state, does the law of cause and effect still apply? If you let go of control and live in a state of being, does being in this state have an effect? Is it right to wait for the effect, or how do we know when to take action?

> MICHAEL: There is a universal law of cause and effect and it is always in operation. It is what the Eastern traditions call karma. It is basically the consequences of our actions (if you do one action, something else is going to happen down the road). The linear nature of this is what most people experience, but when we get to spirit, cause and effect become two sides of the same coin. It is as if the effect can also create the cause. In this part of the book it becomes a circular process, and we want to get out of linear thinking. We want to begin to tear down mental concepts so that we are more centered in our heart space, more centered in the mystical loving space.

In mystical orientation the effect is the cause and the cause is the effect. It is circular in a way that is not going to make sense because with regards to time the past, present and future are all one.

There is the mystical orientation and there is also living in the material world. This means cause and effect does not go away. It is part of reality; it is one of the universal laws. It is useful to pay attention to it—in ourself, in our behaviors, and in the impact our behaviors have on other people and on the world around us. We also need to accept the results of our prior actions which could show up much later.

When we talked about relinquishing control, it is not 100% of the time. There are times when you are working on task and when it is useful to step into your control such as planning an event. It is loosening the attachment to it so that we are not dependent on having to control the world around us. We can control or not control in a flowing way which depends on whatever the moment is calling for. Sometimes when we do relinquish control, the outcome is better than we could have predicted. That is part of living in spirit.

Let's look at a way to work with the principle of using control rather than relinquishing it. We can begin to look more at a particular effect we want to experience and then back-engineer it. This would be intentionally causing an effect to happen. This approach, which we talked about in Part One, works with the present state and desired state in order to intend a particular outcome (or to cause an effect to happen). It works with the present state and desired state in order to intend a particular outcome (or to cause an effect to happen).

For example, we wanted this book to be useful and to resonate with readers. When we were writing, we keep revisiting that vision and intending it to happen. From the intention we back-engineered the content. The intention affected how we wrote the book. By working this way it opened up new vistas to explore and research. With the intention we put the pieces together and the outcome moved in that direction. This is cause and effect—we are causing an outcome to happen by our intention. We never get away from cause and effect but we can use it wisely.

## Working with Suffering

For many people around the world there is intense suffering going on. We need to be able to take this suffering into account and consider how we work with it as human beings. We hope that it never happens to anyone, but if it does, we want to have a way to work with the situation and with how to get through it.

Though it might be painful, it is important to address and examine the experience itself. It is also helpful to realize that sometimes these things operate as a passageway for our growth. There are rites of passage for each of us in life. The passages can be chronological (for instance a midlife transition) or can come from crisis moments. They are opportunities to sit with the experience and see how it is informing us. How is it causing us to grow and mature in a different or new direction?

Maybe in a moment we only feel the suffering. But we can also ask, "How is this suffering contributing to my greater growth as a human being and to my greater well-being?" Then we can begin to work with the experience even though it is difficult and painful. It can often lead us to a new plateau in life—a new frontier—something that we have not yet encountered.

There is the phrase, "It is always darkest before the dawn." Sometimes with these types of experiences that involve intense human suffering it can seem as if there is no benefit. However, we must see that there will be a dawn—that it is something that we will get through and the benefit may come only in hindsight.

For me I think of the loss of my parents and how difficult it was, but it brought me to a new maturity and a new level of responsibility for myself. I come back to the victims of natural disasters. Regardless of what kind of people they were, everyone collectively in that situation had to deal with the loss of their towns and cities—and individually with the loss of their homes. How can they grow from that? I think of victims of war, the refugees, the people who have been displaced, and how a lot of good people suffer. Also, there are the accidents and ailments people face which cause them to endure physical pain. If we encounter this, each of us must work with the challenges that it brings.

How do we hold this? How do we work with these types of experiences, not only for ourselves but also for those around us? They are deeply profound for people and yet a lot of times we do not have meaning as we confront why these things happen. It makes no sense. Why should anyone have to go through this? A lot of times it can lead us to what is called an impasse, where it seems there is no way to get through something.

Yet, if we stay on the edge of it, if we stay working with it, if we stay in the dark before the dawn, eventually the light of the other side begins to emerge. That process sometimes remains hidden. It remains a mystery for people, and that is where faith and trust come in. No matter what you are hitting, there is a way to get through it. There is a way in which Spirit is guiding you through that for your own growth as a human being.

This can be very challenging for a lot of people, and yet it is one of the important aspects of surrender—how do we surrender to these most difficult of human experiences?

MARCEY: For many of us doing this work, we may have certain sensitivities to suffering around us, even to strangers. We are empathetic, so living in a world with suffering is difficult. In 2012, when the Sandy Hook shooting killed twenty-six people at an elementary school, twenty of them were kids in a kindergarten class. At the time our oldest son was only a few months into his kindergarten year and getting ready for the winter holiday break. Like many families across the country, when I heard about the mass shooting, the event took over my life as if it happened in our city. I read about each victim and watched every news story I could. I became overwhelmed with grief for the families and felt enraged at the murderer. It was traumatic for me for weeks. I got stuck in a dark place.

Eventually, I had to force myself to move beyond it and take action where I could. If I would have known at the time to sit with the impact of the tragedy, I think the trauma could have been processed within me with much more love, with less rage and less darkness.

MICHAEL: Yes, suffering is always an invitation for prayer, to send love and well-wishes, or to be inspired to take action. Here's another example. There is a lot of disagreement on which way the country needs to head politically and socially. People feel polarized and oppressed as there is less and less under their control. Yet again here is an opportunity to send out well-wishes and hold a greater consciousness for where we are headed as a society. Maybe positive change is happening on a larger timeframe. Maybe we do not see what is unfolding because we are in the immediate impasse of something that seems like a no win situation for everyone. We have the option to trust that there is a greater spiritual plan unfolding even if it is beyond our awareness.

MARCEY: For me with Sandy Hook, the suffering was very painful and felt so near to me that it drove a need to get involved locally. Even though this tragedy happened somewhere else, my direction to make an impact started my years of volunteering within the community—on behalf of children in the community. There are things within our world that are out of our control, but what is in our control is how we respond. For me it was volunteering, connecting with leadership within our school and the district, being involved in meetings where school safety was discussed, being a support for our teachers and administrative staff, and regular prayer for everyone impacted.

Difficult things happen in our lives, but if you do not accept and eventually surrender to what is, it is possible that the situation will continue to bring uneasiness because you are battling what you want versus what is—and this can create unnecessary pain.

Please remember that no matter what you encounter in your inner experiences, there is also the aspect of acceptance. Emotions such as sadness, frustration, grief and stress may come from not accepting what is because you want things to be different than what they are.

Sometimes when we learn to accept, we feel that it might make it harder. One might suddenly feel the grief, and most people do not want to feel pain or grief. We avoid surrendering because we think we are being strong, or we need to suck it up, or do something that does not necessarily have to be done. Sometimes the surrender and the acceptance will open us up deeper and this can make us feel vulnerable, but this is part of living a spiritual life. You can find a great strength in your ability to be vulnerable.

Let's continue our exploration of trusting your spirit within.

## Taking Risks

It is risky to jump off into the unknown - it is the leap of faith. To take the chance means trusting it is the right direction even though the way forward may be uncertain. For instance, if you start a new business, at the very beginning you will have to takes some risk in terms of financial resources and time commitments. If you maintain a strong intention, your chances of success are much greater and thus there is less risk. If you are always playing it safe, you are probably not going to get out of your comfort zone. In addition to the unknown, change can also feel risky even though it may not be. It might be moving you to a better place in your life, but it can still feel like a risk. Once you build your capacity for risk, it gets easier. You do not need your risk-taking to be foolish or dangerous in any way; it can be prudent. You also have to know for yourself what is a challenge or a risk and what is not necessary or a waste of energy.

If you are risk averse, if you are always looking for comfort, then spirit and its hidden nature can trigger the fight/flight part of your brain. But this does not have to hold you back. You can build your risk tolerance and your experience of safety (remember this from Part Two). You have the ability to explore risk now and then. It does not mean acting foolhardy, but instead finding the ability to get out of your comfort zone.

Let's look at some inquiry to help you feel more internal safety and to build your risk tolerance:

▸ What is your experience when you feel safe?

▸ What would it be like if you could feel this safety even when you take a risk?

▸ What happens for you when spirit and safety are brought together?

MARCEY: When talking about taking risks, there is the duality of not taking chances, staying comfortable, and then taking too much risk because one may be afraid or have a fear of missing out.

MICHAEL: Fear of missing out (FOMO) lets the outer dictate their inner as opposed to the opposite. Examples could be thinking others are having a great time while you are not or thinking that your friends are doing things without you. Fear of missing out is still fear. If you are being fear-driven, it does not matter what the fear is. If you are operating from fear, you are operating from a limited state. Fear begets fear. If your experience is fearful, life will give you more reasons to be fearful. If you feel safe, life gives you more reasons to feel safe even if you are taking a risk.

## Inner Listening/Discerning

*"Intuition is the whisper of the soul."*
~Jiddu Krishnamurti

In trusting spirit we also need to practice inner listening and discerning. Here we define discernment as perception in the absence of judgment with a view to obtaining spiritual guidance and understanding. When asking questions, how do we differentiate between what is authentic inner listening versus the old tapes in your head? What things should we ask internally versus out into the world? When there is a choice of direction to make, which is the best path forward?

### 🔑 KEY DEFINITION

*Discernment: Perception in the absence of judgment with a view to obtaining spiritual guidance and understanding.*

The third guiding question, "What am I really here to do?", also involves the process of discernment. Even though you might feel you are already living your purpose and think you are done with the question, discernment is an ongoing process in living a spiritual life.

Everyone needs to understand their own spiritual language—how does spirit speak to you personally? It opens into the realm of intuition and trusting your intuition. How does one know? There is a kind of inkling or maybe a type of gut feeling. It might feel like a hunch at times, but it has a different quality to it. That is the thread to pull.

I use the metaphor of a treasure hunt. You are trying to find the treasure and you get a few clues. To hear the clues you have to listen closely and pay attention. You have to listen to the little intuitive voices, the hunches, the synchronicities and signposts. Sometimes there is something that shows up internally in your body, in a sensation or in your mind, in a vision or a dream; but sometimes things show up externally—in the people we meet, in synchronicities, in coincidences, in things that can happen around us as well.

This speaks to an overall orientation of listening and beginning to discern.

As you practice it important to stay the course. What is intuition versus something that is leading you astray? You must begin to sort out what is authentic wisdom and what it a folly. Is it guidance coming from your center or deception coming from limiting past programming? Also, it is important to know what your questions are. What are you asking for? What are you working with at any particular time? Your ongoing discernment will keep you on track.

Sometimes your discernment can be a bit of a "dark night of the soul." The phrase is from St. John of the Cross, a fourteenth-century Christian mystic. In the book The Dark Night of the Soul: A Psychiatrist Explores the Connection Between Darkness and Spiritual Growth, the author, Gerald May, lays out quite beautifully that it is not dark in a bad way; it is dark in a hidden way. It is dark in that something is working beyond our awareness. There has to be a trust that involves the inner listening. You are listening into the unknown, listening for something to arise that is a clue or a direction. It sometimes takes time. With discernment, when you are trying to determine a bigger life path, it is a discernment process, which means you are constantly listening to what spirit wants from you. What is the direction of your fulfillment? What is the edge of your awareness about what you are discerning? If you can stay with it, you will begin to get answers. This is also useful when contemplating worldly questions such as a career change or moving your home location.

If you ask your question, stay with it and wait, it will unfold in the living of your life. And yet it brings in a different dimension. It brings a different quality to life and you start to sense the "something more" factor. You start to sense that something greater is at work—in you, around you, and beyond you.

In that respect discernment is a guide itself—the listening process is a guide. This whole book is about inner guidance, but we want to reiterate the most important point for you to really understand—*that the ultimate guide is truly within you.* It is deep within you and it remains hidden a lot of the time.

If you ask, you listen, you pray, and you continue to work with your questions, the guidance comes—it comes out of the listening.

This process is very personal for people. It is also very vulnerable for people because there is no immediate answer, and we each have to bridge that frontier in our own way. We have to know our own edges of our current awareness about the direction we seek. An edge is like the horizon—it is as far as we can see but we sense there is something beyond.

## KEY CONCEPT

*The ultimate guide is truly within you. It may remain hidden, but if you ask, listen, pray and continue to work with your questions, the guidance will come. It comes out of the listening.*

This level of inner listening is not a listening with the ears, but a listening with the heart. We need to be receptive to receiving whatever the guidance is we need. We are putting ourselves in a highly receptive state, then waiting and listening, and knowing that sometimes it takes time. Sometimes we see, hear or feel things, we get a message; and sometimes we are left in the dark for a while. If this occurs, it is what's supposed to be happening. If we are in the dark for a while, then we need to trust that it is part of the discerning, that it is part of the listening, that something is at work beyond our awareness and maybe the timing for our knowing is not right yet. Many times in our discernment we are being asked to hold or to wait.

## Waiting with Patience

*"Have patience with everything that remains unsolved in your heart. Do not despair if the answers don't come immediately. Some answers are only revealed with the passage of time."*
~ Rainer Maria Rilke

Waiting and the quality of how we wait is a huge part of the spiritual journey. Sometimes we are waiting for guidance, sometimes we are waiting for an invitation, sometimes we are waiting for a response. The patience we bring to the quality of our waiting determines a lot.

We need to be patient on the spiritual timing of things because it is not on our time, and we are not in control on that level. The patience can be a joyful waiting for what will eventually arrive in our listening.

In my own process patience is a continual lesson, and in waiting often things do not happen in the timeframe that I want them to happen. When that is the case, I trust that something is happening beyond my awareness. Sometimes I have an intention or I have something I am working with and it does not seem to be happening fast enough. It is a great opportunity to practice patience. Usually something else is happening, something more going on for the greater good, and I am not privy to it yet. Maybe I do not see the ways I am being guided and developed into being a better human being. One of my martial art teachers once used a phrase I often return to: "Don't peek at the rice before it is done; it won't turn out right." The quality of waiting and the patience we have in waiting helps bring our growth and learning to a more complete fulfillment.

## Navigating Pitfalls of Progress

It is important to note that as you get more and more clear, sometimes you begin to have different "psychic" experiences. Many people get fascinated by that. We have to watch our attachment to these kinds of phenomena. Maybe you are going to develop a psychic gift as a result of getting in touch with your deeper nature. However, once you start grabbing at the gifts that come, it starts to be counter-effective. You are then back in a grasping nature and trying to control the process.

Wonderful things can happen, but we want to loosen our attachment to those experiences and allow them to flow freely. Maybe after meditating for a while, you gain a better sense of what other people may be thinking. You think, "Wow, I have got this amazing new gift!" A lot of people can get fascinated by this mind reading and say, "Oh, I am going to focus more and more on that." However, this moves them off track from what got them the gift in the first place - getting still, staying clear, and staying in spirit.

The more we go to that place, the more we sit in that silent place in the heart, strangely, it changes everything on the outside. It changes how we experience and interact with the world around us. That is why we say "no-self" on the inside and "authentic self" on the outside, because it changes the experience of self and what is authentic.

We talked about acceptance and about having a lot of compassion and patience for ourselves as we are going through this process. Our overall development can take time. Maybe we are not going to see the results we want right away, and if we jump ship too soon, we would miss the opportunity. Waiting, patience, and being persistent on our path is critical. Also being committed to your path is crucial. When we are committed fully and engaged with our purpose, it engages a state of provenance. This is where a lot of the magic happens—wisdom, serendipity and coincidence. These are things that we cannot make happen, but seem to happen the more we surrender to spirit. These experiences are wonderful things. Again we want to steer clear of grasping at them, instead we want to see them more as byproducts of our spirit, and always go for the main core of what got us there in the first place.

As we trust spirit more and more each day, we begin to make progress and we begin to see the way the spiritual life can actually work in the world. We start to experience the return to the village.

# CHAPTER 19

▲ ▲ ▲

# Returning to the Village

*"The ordinary can be like medicine"*
~Sherman Alexie

## Correctness in the World

As you begin to listen to the spiritual cues and follow your body rather than your mind, you can explore what is correct or the correct path for your life. If you have trained your mind to follow your body and to let your body be informed by spirit (the mind is informed by spirit too), then you can explore what feels correct for you. It is there that you will find an unequivocal Yes in your body. In the return to the village, or how you live out your life, correctness shows you the way. It transcends having to figure it out with your mind.

What are we talking about when we say correctness?

There is correctness for each of us. We can explore this by asking the following questions: What is the correct choice when you have a decision to make? When you have to be with a certain person, is it correct for your body? Do you feel the proper vibration, the proper energy aligned with your spirit and your lifeforce? In this practice it is never personal if it is not correct even if it means saying no to certain people.

For a lot of people, it has to do with the life force and their energy coming forth—it either will or won't; there is no in-between. We have talked about how there is a kind of binary setting in the body. It is either on or off. Your energy is either coming forth or it is not there.

For example, when you meet someone new, you want to listen to your body's response for what is correct. There is an experience that says, "Okay, am I supposed to spend time with this particular person and not that person?" It is not personal at this level. We are not saying, "I do not like you, so I am not going to spend time with you." We are saying it is not correct and thus not personal.

There is a correct path for your life. In the modality of Human Design, they call it your fractal which is your line of people, places and events that are aligned with who you are in your highest self. As you begin to clarify your vibration, you become more aligned with your communities and the people you are here to connect with.

If you come across someone that is not on your fractal, you might not have any reason to hang out with them. It is not personal; it is rather a different order of things. If you come across someone socially whose energy feels abusive or insincere, you do not need to judge them for that. However, you do not need to hang out with them. They have every right to their experiences and only you can know if is correct for you to interact with them.

That is what correctness is. It is starting to discern and evaluate:

▸ What is correct at a body level for you?

▸ Who is correct for you?

▸ What choices are correct?

As an example, if you want to buy a house and have three different choices, rather than trying to logically evaluate it with pros and cons, you can start to immediately tap into the body and feel which response is the strongest, the most powerful, for the choice you want to make. This is another level of listening to the body, another level of instinct and intuition.

### Exercise

This is an exercise to help you get in touch with what is correct. Generally, in the body there is a clear experience on what is a "yes" and what is a "no."

Think of a person you care deeply about and notice what a "yes" feels like in your body.

Think of a food you dislike intensely and notice what "no" feels like in your body.

Now think of a person or intention—notice how your body responds.

**Explore having someone else ask you questions in a yes or no format.**

**Continue to notice what "yes" or "no" feels like in your gut, pelvis and energetic responses.**

Somehow the body knows everything and every person that is correct by its response. Sometimes it is not clear and maybe on the emotional level you have to mull it over for a while. It might not always be an immediate response from the body. But still, correctness is letting the body lead and listening to what the body tells you is correct. If it's not clear then you must wait and listen for clarity.

> MARCEY: I had a volunteer accounting position at a local nonprofit. I had done it for a couple of years, but it had become more time-consuming and complicated. I had become unhappy spending the time needed to do a good job. When I listened to my body, I realized that this was not my gig—this position was not bringing me joy and excitement and usually ate up time that I could be using on something that got me excited. I reached out to the person in charge to ask about a transition plan. I remembered what I sometimes tell myself: "Just because I can, it doesn't mean I should."

> MICHAEL: This is a good type of selfish. You are following what is correct for yourself. Sometimes it can be hard to be selfish in this way, but remember it is not personal. You can still live your purpose; you can still be kind to people and think of others before self. This is about you tracking the things and people that do and do not reflect you.

> The more you follow what is correct in your body, the more you align with the people, places, events and things that are fulfilling, enjoyable and loving. You start to feel more alive because you are tracking the aliveness response in yourself.

MARCEY: In the past I would have sucked it up, put my feelings aside, and continued to do what was asked of me. The story in my mind would be: "I signed up for this job; I need to put my head down and do the work. Others put in more time than me. Why am I complaining?"

MICHAEL: That is rational justification and that is of the mind. You override your body intelligence when you think that way. The body knows pretty instantly. This way of tracking through the body is a new approach to moving through life, and it is what helps us return to the village. We have the mountaintop experience but the challenge for many people is how to bring that back into the village, how to live it out in the world. That is what correctness helps us do.

## Playing in the Illusion of the World

At this stage we need to understand something about the outer world. It is an illusion projected from within, from the perceptions of what we each consider reality. Life gives you back what you expect from it, both consciously and unconsciously. If reality is an illusion from within, then you can change it from within. When you want to engage purpose and be back in the world, the world becomes like The Matrix from the popular movie series. It operates like one big programmable matrix that can be changed based on one's inner experiences.

This program gives us each what we need in order to experience our lives. The more you follow correctness, the more you can plug into that matrix in a beautiful wonderful way. In the Eastern tradition they call it "The Maya" which is the illusion that we are living in. It is the illusion of the world around us. It is also the illusion of our separateness.

In this part of the book we are bringing it all together by talking about unified consciousness, but we still have to live out our separateness. Once you understand there is another reality behind the separateness, then you can live both. You are living the mystical state, that "something more", and you are living out how your body best plugs into this illusion.

## Proper Timing in Taking Action

As we begin to follow spirit, listen internally, and take action in the world, there is a proper timing as to when to take action. We are looking for an opening or a window in time. What is the exact moment when my action is going to be most effective? Sometimes that means acting immediately; sometimes that means waiting. It's not always jumping immediately into action, but waiting for the right timing, waiting for some signal, a cue or an opening.

How do you know the best moment to jump into action?

It is almost as though a window of opportunity opens and then you jump through it! If you wait for the proper timing, it works like magic, like clockwork. If the timing isn't right, too soon or too late, things may not work out.

This concept comes from the martial arts. In martial arts I practiced a form called Shintaido. When we are practicing attack and receive scenarios, there is a proper timing to receiving your opponent's attack. If your timing is superb, you can move in a relaxed slow state and still beat the other person. We call that "A-timing." If I am too soon, my opponent has time to adapt. If my timing is too late, then I must speed up and rush to deal with the situation. There is a timing that comes from perceiving the right moment but in a different kind of way. The perception and how to sense into that is a different kind of perception.

When we practiced, we explored that timing by learning to sense the other person's intent in our own bodies. When anyone moves their body in any way, there is first an intent in the mind. Then that intent travels in their nervous system, to their muscles, until it transfers into movement. When you get sensitive and open enough, you can actually feel another person's intent. Before they start to move, you can move according to their intent. This means you are already ahead of them once they start their movement.

By analogy we can see that there is a proper timing to our actions. If you are too soon or too late on your timing, you are not going to have the most effective outcome. This may seem like a very nebulous concept. Even during my martial arts practice, it was very nebulous. It is almost like a psychic feeling in your body; this person is about to move, and I act, trusting my body's sense. If they're already moving, I am too late.

What is this little window of proper timing? When is the moment when your action is going to be most effective? If it is too soon or too late, you might not have the best results.

You can begin to track it by noticing your timing in everyday life. Are you showing up right on time? Are you showing up early? Are you running late? If you say, "Oh, I am running late", your timing is not correct. If you are too early to your appointments, then it is also not proper timing.

Being on time is being in the right place at the right time. Notice if you are showing up early or late in your life and explore adjusting your timing. Maybe something is saying, "Not yet." Maybe wait a day or two, a week or two. It is a practice of listening for the impressions by intuiting when is best time to move.

> MARCEY: As an achievement-oriented person I used to beat myself up for not making the date on something or being late with deliverables. What I'm learning is when I experienced a delay and took later action, it ended up being the perfect time and other support or opportunities became available. I am understanding that there won't be bad timing if I can trust my instincts. If everything is perfect, whole and complete, then the timing and decision will not be wrong. I can trust that I will make the best decision at that moment.

## More Explorations of Returning

> MARCEY: I want to go back to the sentence, "Inwardly we need to practice no-self, while outwardly we need to be authentically self." I find this to be a remarkable concept. We have heard of monks that live no-self within communities, so I always thought that mystical goal was the end state of being that no-self person in the village. But it is not that. This connection to no-self happens for me during meditation and quietness, but I am also a body with history, DNA, life force, family, issues, challenges, deficits and gifts. The shift for me is being this individual person in the village while embodying my own inner

connected guide. Those together in combination are unique and distinct for me.

MICHAEL: You have really evolved in your understanding since the beginning of our process! You have your inner guide; that inner no-self. The only way you are going to plug into the matrix correctly, into the outside world, is by referencing it back through your physical reality. You are first removing yourself from reality to go get this clarity, to get to this mystical state. Then you are bringing that back. But you are bringing that back through the medium of yourself, of your authentic self. As you do that, it changes self. This is when (how) you want to apply intuitive inner listening. As that experience of clarity comes through, it changes how you think. It changes your body and the sensations. The subtleties that you begin to notice are different. This is intuitive at a different level. It is a body intuition.

It is different from intuiting with the mind. Not everyone is body-oriented and this is okay. Some of us might need to learn to reference our bodies deeper, but please remember there are many ways to listen. If someone is more mind/thinking oriented, maybe spirit is going to speak to them more through images, visions and dreams versus through the body or emotions. On the emotional level, maybe it is a subtle emotion of love, joy, peace or some other feeling. Maybe spirit speaks more through sensations you feel in your body. The more you can reference the body level the better, but again it is not required. There is no hard or fast rule. Simply notice and feel deeper with more and more clarity. How is the presence of spirit within you coming through you today?

As an example, I am sitting here now doing my inner work. In my inner state I am clear and calm. When I open my eyes and I begin to look out in the world, I notice the flowers are a little bit brighter, the birds are chirping, and there is a sparkle to the sunshine. Spirit can affect your senses; it can affect your feeling and thinking. Begin to notice things at a different level of reality-events that are happening that you have not been paying attention to.

MARCEY: I am still trying to learn about listening to my body (after many years of not listening to it). What I am learning is that one way to listen to my body is through what we might call instinct and starting to trust that instinct as an inner guide. It seems that instinct may be somewhat of a medium for how spirit speaks through one's body.

MICHAEL: It is an instinct, a kind of primal intelligence in your body. Remember that our bodies know way more than our minds do. If you begin to trust and follow that instinct, it will be part of your inner guide. It is more of a subtler listening into the body. As you go deeper, your body gets more and more sensitive.

You can notice more of the subtle aspects of these sensations and experiences in your body. As spirit informs your body, it changes. As you do body practices such as tai chi or yoga, you clear the energy channels in the body (the meridians in Chinese medicine and the nadis in yoga). You begin to feel more. As you feel more, you feel more of the subtlety beneath everything. You become more and more sensitive to that subtly. Yet that subtlety seems to be more profound and impactful.

In order to notice at a more subtle level, it is necessary to refine how you listen to your body. In the practice of proper timing your body may say, "Now is the time to move. This moment is the proper time." That moment might come and go if you are not paying attention or haven't learned to recognize the feeling. There will be a moment when the instinct speaks and you need to listen for that.

A lot of times when we are starting a project or jumping into something there is great enthusiasm at the beginning. However, many times that initial burst begins to fade. It might not be the energy we need to get us through the entire project. We might need to listen more deeply for the energy that will sustain our endeavors. It is usually wise to pause before you feel the urge to tear into something. Are you ready to begin? Are your ducks in line? Is your action coming from the right place and is it the proper timing? Again check in with yourself. Are you trying to leap too soon or have waited too long on taking action?

## Holding Space

When we talk about holding space, this is something we can learn to do for others in our life. This is an aspect of caring for the people around us, by listening, by receiving, and by what I call "holding space." When you practice this, it is as if you are surrounding others with space.

When you hold space for others, you temporarily halt your own reactions, you temporarily halt the relational aspect, and you enter into the mystical space. You hold that space on behalf of yourself and the other person in the relationship. I called it holding space because you are holding or creating the mysti-

### 🗝 KEY CONCEPT

*Holding space for others gives the other person our undivided attention and allows us to be fully present in another aspect of ourselves.*

cal space, and allowing the other person to be present without a reaction to them. No matter what goes on for them, you allow it to occur and you do not have a relational reaction to it. When you're done holding space, you can always go back to reacting.

Holding space does not mean doing this 100% of the time because we do not want to ignore the authentic relationship. But this is a tool and a gift that we can employ when we need to have empathy, when we need to see that the other person needs to have their experience without interference. We give them the space to be and to experience whatever they will.

> MARCEY: Learning to hold space is a useful practice that I have learned from you. First, I see that person as their whole and complete self. That opens up the space

and puts me in a mindset, a certain energy, and opens up my heart. I no longer drive the conversation. Instead, I am more encircling them in a safe space—one with love and open-heartedness.

MICHAEL: This also relates to presence which we talked about earlier. It is a similar concept—holding space and being very, very present with the people in the world around us.

When we hold space, we are not interfering in any way, but it does have an effect on the other person because they are getting undivided attention. When someone is on the receiving end of that, it is usually a positive experience for them. In our day-to-day life we normally are not giving our full attention to others. This is also a dimension of unconditional love. When we practice unconditional love for ourselves and others by holding space, it allows us to be present in another aspect of ourselves.

## Exercise

The next time you are around someone you care about, see if you can listen without responding and simply pay attention to them; simply hold space for them while being as present as you can.

# CHAPTER 20

▲ ▲ ▲

# Moving Toward Differentiated Unity
# —A Collective Vision for Humanity

In a greater vision for humanity everyone has a part to play. In this greater vision we can contemplate the concept of "interconnectedness." Once we start to move back out in the world with our purpose, we move to an interconnected state. Interconnectedness means we are also interdependent. This is very different from codependent.

In Part One we discussed codependency as it relates to empowerment. If we continue with that theme, there are three stages to the empowerment journey: from 1) codependent to → 2) independent (empowered as an individual) to → 3) interdependent (empowered as an individual within a group).

When we are *interdependent*, we value interacting with the people around us. We still need other people because we are not operating in an isolated place. We begin to take others' experiences into account and reflect on how our own behavior and communication is affecting those around us. Further, we can start to sense more of a collective consciousness, something greater that everyone gets to participate in. That "something greater" consciousness includes you and is also within you. In this level of consciousness your purpose is always being done through you rather than you doing it. Imagine if everything you do becomes source acting through you.

We can also imagine that in this collective vision, we have some place where humanity is headed as a whole. We do not know what that is. We could say it is utopia or heaven on earth, but having a utopian vision for humanity is not realistic, nor practical. However, it is still a nice way to view this collective vision, this something greater for humanity.

## Moving from Symbiotic to Unified

As individuals when we experience our separateness, it can cause us to feel alone. In those times there is an urge in many people to go back to the womb, to go back to a symbiotic state in order to gain nurturing. The symbiotic state is unitive, but not differentiated; we did not have our individuality in that state. We were one with everything, but we did not have any sense of separateness.

We had to move out of that state so we could know ourselves as individuals. We had to develop our ego to know ourselves as separate. That brought us to the pain of separateness. How do we deal with that? We need to continue our journey and move into something greater than just self. We need to move to our place in the greater vision.

This brings us to a differentiated unity versus the undifferentiated unity of the symbiotic state. In the differentiated unity we hold on to our separate identity while we also experience our place in greater collective consciousness.

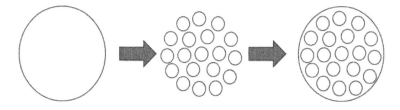

In the **symbiotic state** it is represented by the empty circle. We are one with everything, but have no sense of self.

Then we each go to the **ego state** where we are one of the smaller circles, separate from others individuals (we have self and know our separateness).

In the **unified state** each of the separate egos come together in a greater whole. In the unified state they do not give up their separateness to be part of that collective. This happens through interdependence.

I am living in spirit, but I still need you. We are interdependent on each other in this process, in these relationships. I don't actually need you, but if I am living in something greater, then I do because we are all in life together. We all need each other for the greater reality. It becomes a way of life.

When attempting to move to a higher level of spiritual evolution, a lot of people mistakenly follow the urge to go back to this symbiotic state. They want the warmth and comfort of the womb. When we can understand that drive to go backwards, it helps us move forward.

I think it is a collective theme for humanity: that we are moving toward this way of being able to stay separate but be part of a greater whole.

It means then that we become aware of the value of each individual to this greater whole. No one person can drive the whole vision for humanity, only the part they are called to play. The key is interconnectedness, interdependency... feeling that everyone is a part of a greater collective consciousness and that we all belong.

Imagine humanity as one being, like a grove of trees which share a similar consciousness. Humanity could begin to operate that way; we could begin to operate in some greater "we" consciousness. If we do not learn to cooperate and work together, we run the risk of mass suffering for many of our brothers and sisters.

Aspen trees grow as a community; they are interconnected by their roots and share nutrients and resources to support each other. Underneath they are survivors. An aspen's roots can remain dormant for years. At the right time they jump to life and regenerate as a community. Aspen trees set a community example. If you imagine all of 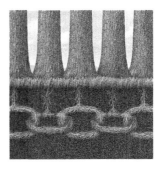 humanity, every human as a tree in that grove, our roots are connected and talking. We are like one organism.

MARCEY: When I feel like I am working and living as my authentic "Marcey", it gives space for others to be their most authentic self. Since what happens on the outside reflects the inside, if we can find peace within and live in that energy, it leaves space for others to do the same. I like the analogy of a forest or grove of trees, showing the trees above and their overlapping roots below. The trees may be different heights, different sizes, different shapes, bend differently, but there is connectedness. They are using the same resources within this big ecosystem. They all get different light from the sun and have different needs, but are part of the same system.

MICHAEL: They can also transfer nutrients to other trees through the mycelium layer in the ground. The mycelium is a layer of interconnectedness in the soil where the different species are communicating with each other in terms of health. They end up supporting each other, and we can do the same thing. Interconnection is normal for nature.

When you see a flock of birds and they move together, how do they know how to move in one larger unit? They are listening to the group energy or the group mind. There is the individual mind and then there is the group mind or group consciousness. Every once a while you will see a bird that will fly off on its own, but mostly they listen to where the whole flock is going and follow that. They seem to do that beautifully. It is the same way with humanity. Where is our flock going? Sometimes it seems as if we are headed off a cliff while at other times we work together with an amazing flow.

Consider tapping into the concept of a team spirit or group mind if we want to get something done. If we want to take on bigger collective challenges such as climate change or people starving around the planet, we need to stop getting personal about it. We may not feel called to work on each issue directly, but we have to begin to see the bigger picture. We have to see that the ills of humanity are only going to get corrected when we start to think collectively, when we start to get beyond the selfishness and the self-absorbed nature of human beings.

It is very difficult because we are by nature self-absorbed—each of us. Life has pushed us. The survival aspect says that it is not wise for me to think about the greater picture when I have my own needs to meet. Practically speaking, you do first have to meet your own needs before you can have the privilege of launching off into a bigger humanitarian vision (remember Maslow's hierarchy of needs that we discussed in Part One).

However, once your basic needs are met, at what point do you have enough? At what point do you know who you are? At what point does it no longer need to be about you? Do you want to be a part of something greater? Do you want to feel a movement for the benefit of the world?

For any movement to be successful, it has to have a greater purpose and the members of the movement must understand this. Many of the movements in our past were trying to make positive change, though often one very important principle was off track. I think they were missing the mark because there was too much ego involved within the participants. Those involved were not able to get over themselves in order to see that they each needed to unselfishly do their part.

In the most successful movements separate individuals do not direct where it is going. These movements have their own energy and momentum to them. It is as if there are no individuals at the helm. Rather than a hierarchal nature, we might consider a more horizontal nature where everyone has a say. It is not communism; we are not saying that I have to give away what I have so that you can have too—that is different. It is saying that there is too much ego in the world. While we still need effective leadership, we do not need anyone at the top telling us what to do. What we need is everyone listening to their inner spirit, to how we get along and how we are going to make it through the collective challenges which confront us together. Each person that does this must personally keep their own ego in check and operate for the greater good.

As we begin to do our spiritual work, as we begin to awaken to the spirit within us, that is what is going to save humanity. It is not going to happen from the outside. We could say that *spiritual evolution* (as opposed to revolution) is something that is happening collectively inside each person.

When we can get over ourselves, we can each play the roles we are called to play based on our passions and interests. We can follow the inner truth of where we need to go. I am not called to go to Africa and help poor villages implement new water systems (although for me that would be a really cool thing to do). However, someone is called to that and it helps the collective. Part of my calling is to connect deeply with the people I support, to put out this book and touch the people I do. This is one way I am plugging in.

It is a higher calling. Imagine a vision where people work together like the parts in a car. The parts have to work together for the car to move effectively. In a collective consciousness someone is going to be the cook, someone the musician, someone the chief, and someone the doctor. Each person has a role to play based on their passions and what they are good at, what they are interested in. The vision, if we can see it, is that we will eventually come together in a beautiful way that will get humanity through these greater collective challenges we are facing.

We have one final point to make.

Consider the term "full enlightenment." It is called a full unitive experience of God in the Judeo-Christian lexicon. This is when we are one with everything, with all that exists in the universe. We need to live out our separateness, but this is living in the illusion, playing in the matrix. Although we experience the illusion of our separateness, we are not separate. We are one with everyone and everything. For each of us we may be lucky if we glimpse this for even an instant. If we do, our whole perspective changes and life is never the same again. Personally, I can't say if I have or have not had this experience. I have had many small enlightenments, but I am never certain I have had this full enlightenment. Maybe? Yet this uncertainty is exactly what keeps me moving in the right direction and keeps me continuing to do the inner work. It is moving us all toward our place in the collective vison for humanity.

There is one more aspect of the Unitive Experience that we have not yet discussed. This is the ability to have unconditional love within our relationships, groups and communities.

# CHAPTER 21

▲ ▲ ▲

# You Are So Loved–Love is Your True Identity

L et's talk about love! We have talked about the mystical space and we can also call it love. It is the still spaciousness, that mystery at the center of your being.

When we get deep into our center, love becomes a mystery. It becomes part of our identity in a spiritual sense. We have our individual identities, but we also have within us an interconnectedness. It is a "oneness" where we are one with everyone and everything—one large self.

If you begin to reference what it is like to feel love, or have an identity when you know we are lovable, then you are referencing your true identity.

Love is what you are made of. It is what allows the parts of your human experience to come together. In terms of your identity and what we learned earlier; this is the part of your identity that is most true but can be difficult for your mind to get around. Your mind might have trouble embracing the totality of your loving nature. It is too big and it is too grand.

In the end our purpose is to know ourselves as love. To really know our own loving identity and to begin to operate from that place. Consider also your behaviors, how would love operate? How would you communicate with the people in your life from this place? How would you hold yourself and others in pleasurable and painful moments?

This love begins to have its own intelligence, its own way of operating and communicating that is always based, as we talked about in the introduction, in wellness. It is always based in inclusion. It is always based in everyone belonging as they are.

MARCEY: This reminds me to remember that we are really never alone. We each have impact on others and others impact us. We have physical connectedness—also spiritual, emotional, energetic and human connectedness—not only to those around us now, but people who came before us, people who will come after us. This is transcendent.

MICHAEL: It can spin in many different directions because love is the mystery at the center of our being. Once we are in the territory of mystery, all bets are off, right? That is the "something more". It is that part that we cannot bring definition to, but it is there in operation.

MARCEY: Sometimes love sounds like a powerless gushy sentimental word, but there are many examples of the strength of coming from love. Love can make you more physically, emotionally and mentally in a place of greater strength and power.

MICHAEL: I think love is a true power, a power beyond worldly power. When we talk about love here, it is not emotional, romantic, nor brotherly love and yet includes them all. We could say it is the ultimate power.

It is it the space that contains and includes the different dimensions of love. It is like a diamond with many, many facets on it. Sometimes we look at one facet and say, "love is romantic love" or "it is brotherly love", but it is so multidimensional that as human beings we cannot understand the full scope of love and what it really is.

It is in us and it is our center, but I think what causes so much challenge for people is the mind cannot get around it. Again it is too grand; it is infinite and eternal.

MARCEY: Is this kind of love the same as faith or what people call God or spirit?

MICHAEL: Yes, you could call it God, you could call it oneness, you could call it enlightenment. This love is the experience of no experience. It is the container that lets us have all human experience. In and of itself it is infinite. It remains undefined, infinitely spacious, and eternally connected.

I like the term love, but again this is not those other kinds of human love; this is unconditional love. Humans can get to it, but it is very challenging for any human being to embody unconditional love because most of the time our love is conditional. What we are talking about here is the love that is completely unconditional, that embraces everyone and everything.

MARCEY: Is it something that you cannot see but know it is there like gravity?

MICHAEL: Yes, that is a beautiful analogy. You can understand what it is; you know it is there; you cannot control it and you do not have power over it.

As a final exploration how do you experience your mountaintop, your loving self in the village?

It is remembering the presence of this love is available to be the place you come from every day. You are love. It is your true identity. This is the final key to achieving the mountaintop experience and living it in your return to the village.

 **KEY CONCEPT**

*You are love.*
*Love is your true identity.*

## Let's recap the key concepts from Part Three:

» Once you know who you are, then you begin to know what you are really here to do.

» As you continue to explore your mystical "center", your purpose unfolds.

» When you are able to sit in the still, empty space, that is your mountaintop. It has its own intelligence. This state becomes your inner guide.

» The key to presence is allowing something greater to come through your individuality.

» If we can be in the yearning, in the desire for something without trying to fill it up, it opens up its own experience as a mystical state.

» The ultimate guide is truly within you. It may remain hidden, but if you ask, listen, pray and continue to work with your questions, the guidance will come. It comes out of the listening.

» Practice no-self on the inside and "authentic self" on the outside.

» Holding space for others gives the other person our undivided attention and allows us to be fully present in another aspect of ourselves.

» You are love. Love is your true identity.

# Conclusion

In the introduction we talked about the need to go inward and why someone would choose to look inward. Throughout the book we tackled some of life's most difficult questions: Who am I? What am I? What am I here to do? In the end you were reintroduced to your true nature—that you are love.

Now it is time for you to take this inward reflection, and as you project it outward into your daily life, watch what transforms as you live life through a new perspective. To that end we have given you as much input as possible given the scope of this book. Below are some of the main points to recall, but know that the answers always lie inside of you.

## Main Points to Remember

The following is a list of the main points. It might not be complete because it needs your own additions of what is important for you or of any new insights you have had. Feel free to add any points you think should be included:

▸ Your best guide through life lies within you—it is part of your spiritual nature. Learn to hear how it speaks to you.

▸ You are whole and complete as you are; nothing is broken and nothing needs fixing. Your pain points are opportunities to go deeper and reach your center. Your center is within and the source of that which you seek and desire. Your true identity is Love.

▸ Your purpose is an expression of who you are. Once you know who you are, then your purpose begins to unfold naturally.

▸ The outer and the inner are one. The outer is a reflection of your inner world and a projection from within. The outer circumstances you encounter are often a result of the inner states you create in your mind.

▷ It is not what you are aware of but what you are not aware of that is holding you back. Becoming conscious of the unconscious is key to your awakening. Notice what is happening below the surface of everyday awareness in order to be able to shift your experiences.

▷ Getting to your mountaintop is important so you can know and understand this experience for yourself. Just as important is your return to the village—how you live your mountaintop in everyday life.

▷ Your mind and body are not separate; your spirit is not separate. Your mind and body and spirit are one. Further, you are not separate from others. Your individuality is one with all humanity. In experiencing and living from this place of unified consciousness, all life becomes sacred, all life becomes holy, because you are always one with it. Everyone is connected and whole as they are.

## Your Ongoing Journey

Reading this book, in and of itself, could be considered a mountain-top experience. When you are finished and you return to the village, integrating the learning into your everyday life is key to your success. Continue to manifest the clarity of this information into your life so that you are learning more as you progress –learning how to be your own guide and how to live in a conscious way.

As a gentle reminder, when you do this work, you may go through periods of time where you feel you have mastered it and everything is flowing—synchronicities are showing up in your life. Then something happens. You get triggered or the flow seems to come to a screeching halt. If this occurs, it is an invitation to again look within. Continue to notice triggers or buttons—being aware so you can dive in and see what is really happening. This way of inner reflection is not an endpoint but a beginning or a signpost along your path. Once in a while you may trip on something, but that is okay. The tools stay the same but the power of this approach always lies in your hands.

Thus, the work needs to be ongoing with courage to blaze your own path as your own guide. In the introduction we said it was a lifestyle, a way of being in the world. Continue to find ways to integrate this approach into your life and gain clarity each and every day.

We highly recommend developing a body practice (yoga, martial arts, tai chi, etc.) and/or a mediation practice (Vipassana, Zazen, prayer, contemplation, etc.). Find time to simply sit and reflect on your interior life. You can also refer back throughout the book and integrate the tools as regular practices.

And of course, getting assistance is crucial.

It is important to know when to reach out and connect to others for support. We recommend participating in workshops and retreats where there are like-minded people, living a conscious life together and supporting each other on the journey. Examining the deeper parts of your unconscious needs conscious relationships. If you'd like to explore our support avenues, here are some ways you can continue with us:

- Individual Private Sessions
- Workshops & Retreats (Online and live)
- Additional Materials
- Social Media
- Video content

For more information on working with these Inside Guide resources and with Michael (and/or Marcey), see the contact information in the next section below.

While fostering a sense of empowerment to do the work yourself, also creating community and bringing people together is key. Having a community as a resource is important. For example, find people, friends, and support whom you can call if you are in need or simply want an outside perspective. Having someone to bounce something off of is helpful—sometimes a buddy system or someone from your peer group.

It is insightful and encouraging to continue the dialogue. "This is where I am still getting triggered" or "this is where I am seeing these amazing new mystical manifestations in my daily life." Sharing challenges and obstacles, as well as wins and breakthroughs, with someone who can also experience this new way of being can be a great addition to your life.

In everyday life we usually do not have a context to talk about mystical experiences. When you begin to meet others and form friendships and community around this type of work, it is amazing to share when something synchronistic happens especially when it is not an everyday occurrence. Eventually, the mystical and rare starts to become more normal. Your support people might share, "Oh, yeah, that happened to me too!"

You start to be able to communicate and interact with a new language and new experiences under your belt. For some people this could be a new sensitivity. Once it is turned on, you may become more intuitive—which could be magical, but also a little uncomfortable as you notice more of the unconscious aspects of life. Different types of mystical experiences may occur such as clairvoyance or empathic abilities. Again, as a precaution, do not focus on having these, but they may occur as a byproduct of doing the work. Simply notice and listen if that is the case. It is your inner guide speaking to you.

As you move forward with this work, keep in mind not to proselytize. It is not useful to be a preacher to the people in our lives, but a living example, a role model. You may find that people inquire when they notice something is shifting in you by asking, "How is that happening for you?" That may be the opening or the opportunity to expose more people in your life to this kind of work. Always trust your inner guidance on what is correct by waiting for the right moment to share.

Spreading consciousness on the planet, person to person and through word of mouth, has always been a part of our human evolution. When we do the inner work with someone, they also become more conscious and then the people in their life are also positively impacted; it is a ripple effect. It is like a pebble in a pond—waves of consciousness traveling out in all directions. The more people we touch with our new awareness and mountaintop energy, the more we are living our purpose. When we do this, we all become happier, more aware, and more awake. The more we touch those around us, the more we can change the world through the relationships we are enhancing.

## We Want to Hear from You!

Send some love back our way:

- ‣ We would love to hear about your experience of reading this book and about your breakthroughs. We encourage you to send us your stories and we will keep you involved in our ongoing dialogue.

- ‣ Please leave a review on Amazon or wherever you purchased The Inside Guide.

- ‣ To stay connected and up to date, follow us on social media and visit our website.

We greatly appreciate you!

## Contact Information:

Website:  **www.loveguides.us**
Email:    **info@loveguides.us**
Facebook: **https://facebook.com/loving.presence.embodiment/**
Instagram: **https://instagram.com/loving_presence_embodiment/**
LinkedIn: **https://linkedin.com/in/lovingpresenceembodiment/**

## A Final Blessing

Our wish is that you remember your true nature as loving presence, that this is your true identity. In the end this is the most accurate description of your essence: a presence of Love embodied, having human experiences. We invite you to live in a state of gratitude. We thank you, our reader, for being willing to take this journey. Thank you for knowing yourself as Loving Presence. Thank you to your Spirit, the true guide within you. Your presence is a joy and gift to the world and the world awaits you!

# About the Authors

## Michael DiPietro

For over 20 years Michael DiPietro has been guiding individuals and groups to overcome obstacles and awaken to authenticity, fulfillment, and life purpose. He has a B.S. degree in Engineering, is a certified Master Practitioner of Neuro- Linguistic Programming, a Martial Art Instructor, skilled bodyworker, meditation teacher and has spent time in both Buddhist and Benedictine Monasteries. Through his extensive training and deep intuition, he guides clients and readers to truly know themselves, to transform challenges, to find meaning and to live their life purpose. He lives in the San Francisco Bay Area.

## Marcey Donnelly

Marcey Donnelly has a 30-year professional career in finance and is currently a Senior Vice President at a leading financial institution. She began in Customer Service and worked her way up by mastering skills in process improvement, leadership, communication, facilitation and project management, as well as delivering multi-million dollar changes to her organization. She studied Advertising at San Jose State University and is Certified in Six Sigma Design (process improvement). In her personal life, Marcey has a passion for helping others. Her volunteer roles have included President of the Parent Teacher Association at two schools, President of Business Network International for her local chapter and several positions at the Boys Scouts of America. She has been a regular volunteer at Hay House events. She is a Professional Member at the International Center for Reiki Training and a certified Reiki Master. Marcey lives in the San Francisco Bay area with her husband and two children.

Made in the USA
Middletown, DE
28 April 2023

29328465R00156